D0016599

Praise for
Making Your Money Count

The kingdom of God wants the God of the kingdom to invade every aspect of your world. In *Making Your Money Count*, Dr. Kenneth C. Ulmer will both instruct and illustrate for you how to turn your financial dreams into your fulfilled destiny. When you finish this book, you will view your wealth from God's perspective, and prosperity will have a life-changing purpose.

Rev. Sunday Adelaja
Senior Pastor and Founder
Embassy of God
Kiev, Ukraine

It is said that among all the parables in the Bible, two-thirds of them speak to the issue of money. We all grapple with the question of how to be good stewards of our resources. What a blessing it is that Bishop Kenneth Ulmer has written a practical guide on the subject based on God's Word. Thank you, Bishop!

Angela Bassett and Courtney B. Vance
Actress/Actor

In *Making Your Money Count*, Dr. Kenneth Ulmer clearly articulates biblically sound truth on the topic of money. I'm amazed at how often the subject of money is misinterpreted and distorted, but Dr. Ulmer brings us back to what the Bible really has to say on money and how we should use what we have. Dr. Ulmer is a great teacher, preacher, man of God and also a great personal friend. Pick up this book and prepare to be changed!

John Bevere
Author and Speaker
Cofounder, Messenger International
Colorado Springs/Australia/United Kingdom

Dr. Ulmer is one of the most strategic Christian leaders in the nation. His impact in helping people understand God's principles for life is enriching while remaining biblical. It is hard to overstate the impact Dr. Ulmer makes on tens of thousands of Christians every week. This is a man who is truly on fire for Christ and longing to help others grow in Him.

Mark Brewer
Senior Pastor, Bel Air Presbyterian Church
Los Angeles, California

Making Your Money Count is about godliness, obedience, trust, maturity and biblical wisdom. Dr. Kenneth C. Ulmer has gathered scriptural evidence and exegeted the text as well as the context. In this book, he will lead you to a comprehensive understanding of how God views all things *you*. Read and grow into all that God purposes for you.

Dr. Samuel R. Chand
Leadership Development Consultant

The greatest law in God's universe is sowing and reaping, especially in the area of money. In *Making Your Money Count,* Dr. Kenneth C. Ulmer clearly teaches us how to move from spending to investing and from seeing what money can do to what money represents in our lives. If you truly want to achieve God's destiny in the years ahead, this invaluable resource is a must-read.

Dr. James O. Davis
Cofounder, Global Pastors Network
Billion Soul Initiative Ambassador
Orlando, Florida

Ken Ulmer is a trusted friend, and *Making Your Money Count* is a written testimony of his life and practice. As one who deeply loves and serves the Lord, Ken writes with authority and passion. You will be encouraged, challenged and blessed as you apply these simple yet often misunderstood and neglected teachings presented in this book.

Max Ellzey
Chairman, The C12 Group
Los Angeles, California

Don't make the mistake of thinking that this book is going to be preachy and impractical! Kenneth Ulmer is keenly aware of what it takes to make your money count. Make friends with this book if you want to manage your resources successfully.

Teresa Hairston
Publisher and CEO, *Gospel Today* magazine

In *Making Your Money Count*, we're given a solid resource from a leader who provides us with the whole package: a book written by a wise pastor, a balanced teacher, a thorough-going scholar, a Bible-preacher and a passionate and godly man. It's a special delight to commend this even-handed, insightful and practical tool that untwists a subject that's too often mangled by poor exposition or distorted by exaggeration. You have to be happy when stewarding our finances is made alive and done right!

Jack W. Hayford
President, Foursquare Churches International
Chancellor, The King's College and Seminary
Founding Pastor, The Church On The Way

Making Your Money Count is a *rhema* word for the Body of Christ. Bishop Kenneth Ulmer counters the critic's question of whether God wants us to be rich with solid fundamental truths found throughout the Bible. This book is astounding and is certain to teach and empower God's children and critics as well.

Bishop Eddie L. Long
New Birth Baptist Church
Atlanta, Georgia

In *Making Your Money Count*, Dr. Ken Ulmer does what he does best. He slices through the confusion, misunderstanding and misinformation and then clearly and accurately explains the Scripture. Satan does not want you to read this book because hell will be plundered, heaven will be populated and you will be blessed and be a blessing!

Robert Morris
Senior Pastor, Gateway Church
Bestselling Author, *The Blessed Life*

Bishop Kenneth Ulmer is one of the truly great spiritual leaders of our time. In this powerful and penetrating book, Bishop Ulmer plumbs the depths of the biblical meaning of prosperity. He confronts the false teaching of both the divine right presumption and the anti-prosperity predispositions in contemporary Christianity. Here is a benchmark book by a dynamic scholar preacher that is inspiring and instructive.

Dr. Lloyd John Ogilvie
Former Chaplin, United States Senate

"A false balance is an abomination to the LORD, but a just weight is His delight" (Proverbs 11:1). In the Scriptures, there are only 500 verses on prayer but more than 2,000 on abundance, money and prosperity. In *Making Your Money Count,* Dr. Ulmer masterfully unravels the divine path to wealth from God's perspective. This is a must-read for all those who are serious in honoring God with their wealth.

Dr. Robb Thompson
President and CEO, Excellent Funding

Making Your Money Count

Kenneth C. Ulmer, Ph.D.

From Gospel Light
Ventura, California, U.S.A.

Published by Regal Books
From Gospel Light
Ventura, California, U.S.A.
Printed in the U.S.A.

Library of Congress Cataloging-in-Publication Data
Ulmer, Kenneth C.
Making your money count / Kenneth C. Ulmer.
p. cm.
ISBN 978-0-8307-4376-6 (hard cover)
1. Money—Religious aspects—Christianity. 2. Finance, Personal—Religious aspects—Christianity. I. Title.
BR115.W4U46 2007
241'.68—dc22

2007006411

1 2 3 4 5 6 7 8 9 10 / 10 09 08 07

Dedication

This book is dedicated to my wife of over 30 years, Togetta S. Ulmer. Togetta is the apple of my eye, the beat of my heart and the wind beneath my wings. All that I am in the natural is because the Lord has loved me through this great woman of God. Togetta and I have learned many lessons about mishandling, handling, mismanaging and properly managing money. Neither of us comes from affluence, but we have always known the Lord as Jehovah Jireh, the Lord who provides. When I have struggled with the ego and economics of being a husband and priest of my family, her encouragement and fidelity were pillars of strength that carried me through such moments of insecurity. When I could not pay our rent in the small apartment we called our first home, she never flinched in her faith in God nor in me. Together we are living testimonies to the fact that God is faithful to do exceedingly abundantly above all we could ever ask or imagine as we follow and trust Him in all ways.

I dedicate this book to my grandchildren: Kamryn, Ayari, Raegan, Bailey, and the one we haven't named yet! Through you, precious children, I have been "born again" for a second time! You motivate me to fulfill the biblical exhortation that "a good man leaves an inheritance to his children's children" (Prov. 13:22). May Papa's life inspire you with a legacy of sowing into the lives of others. Never forget: You are blessed so that you may be a blessing.

I dedicate this book to my children, RoShaun, Keniya, Kendan and Jessica, who have shared me with so many others. You are my beloved son and daughters in whom I am well pleased.

And I dedicate this book to my mother, Ruth Naomi Ulmer, whose life has been one of making money count. She clings to a life well lived, no longer being able to recall the vast sacrificial investments she made into my life. I am eternally grateful for her model of money management.

Every time I walked across a stage to receive a degree, I tearfully recalled the invaluable investment she made in the lives of her children. I have slept in hotel rooms around the world, recalling how she cleaned bathrooms and changed beds for wealthy people who trafficked in circles she never knew, but in which I have walked as her vicarious representative. I have gone where she could not, because of her ability to use money as a tool to invest in my life and in the lives of others. Her ability to stretch a dollar—with class and elegance—often made me wonder if perhaps she possessed miraculous powers!

This book is dedicated to the dozens of young men and women who were blessed by my mother's generosity. This book is a testimony to the hours she spent cleaning other people's houses while transforming hers into a godly home. May her investment in me extend as an investment to you as you read this book.

Contents

Section III: Economics 101

Section IV: Moving Forward

FOREWORD

In an age obsessed with money, *Making Your Money Count* raises one's thinking above the common attitude of the culture: The rich get richer and the poor want to become rich in order to catch up with the rich. Here, to address that defeating quandary, comes a fantastic book that is the most positive collection of principles of how to lift people from degrading poverty into self-esteem-generating prosperity by a specific process that reveals God's mind-set concerning our financial affairs.

Poverty in a land of plenty stands as a stark reality of life alongside the poverty of economically depressed and oppressed governments. This work suggests that the greatest lack is the lack of understanding of the purpose of money. You will be challenged to look beyond the process of wealth accumulation to the purpose of wealth acquisition.

Financial gurus, late-night hawkers of packaged get-rich plans and icons of financial success all appear to focus the attention of the observer on quick strategies to "get all you can and can all you get." Today's culture is characterized by a certain level of insensitivity to the needs of others that is dwarfed by a narcissistic obsession with self. It is within this context of cultural "me-ism" that you will be challenged to rethink your personal philosophy of money. You will be encouraged to look beyond poverty to provision and to then see purpose.

If you deal with money—whether you are rich, poor or in between—this book is for you. If you want to learn how to ease your monetary struggles, open your life to the benefits of God's financial blessings and help others who may be struggling financially, this book shows you how. The principles and biblical insight it contains are right on.

Dr. Kenneth Ulmer is one of a select group of pastor friends from whom I receive great inspiration. I would urge anyone who wants to know God's process for lifting people from poverty to financial productivity and wise money management to read this book! It contains new thinking on a psychological and biblical foundation that I applaud.

Dr. Robert H. Schuller
Crystal Cathedral
Garden Grove, California

The Choice Is Yours

This is what the LORD says: "Take your choice."

1 CHRONICLES 21:11, *NIV*

Albert Einstein once said, "I am convinced that God does not play dice." Einstein was right. God doesn't have to gamble—He knows the beginning from the end. But that's not to say He has never taken a gamble. In fact, one of the biggest gambles God took when He created humans was to give us *choice*. It was a gamble because He placed fully into our hands the choice to believe in Him or not. The choice to treat our fellow human beings with kindness or not. The choice to follow His ways or not. The choice to trust and obey Him or not.

He gave us choice because He didn't want little robots running around programmed to worship Him—He desired true fellowship with His creation, fellowship that is real, not forced.

If there are a number of different choices to make in any given situation, then that would seem to indicate that there are any number of possible outcomes, depending on the choice we make. If we are choosing blind, with no wise guidance or proven process to follow, then we diminish our chances of making the right decision. Still, we get to choose.

Giovanni Pico della Mirandola, an Italian Renaissance philosopher, wrote in *Oration on the Dignity of Man*, "Thou shalt have the power to degenerate into the lower forms of life, which are brutish. Thou shalt have the power, out of thy soul's judgment, to be reborn into the highest forms, which are divine."[1] That "power," that choice, is a gift from God. It all begins with choice, and He watches us every moment, observing every decision we make.

Because He loves us so much, God wants to assist us in making choices that will give us every possible chance to experience only the best, His best: the most peaceful, the most productive, the most positive outcomes we could possibly experience during our brief time here on Earth. For that reason, He gave us His Word, the Bible, in order to provide us with guidance, instructions, processes and commands on how to live our lives and how to deal properly with every conceivable situation we might encounter. And although He wants us to follow the ways that He has laid out for us, God never forces us to do so, even when our experiences inform us in hindsight that His ways are always best for our ultimate happiness and success. This is because He loves us so much that He wants only the best for us. "I chose you and appointed you that you should go and bear fruit, and that your fruit should remain, that whatever you ask the Father in My name He may give you" (John 15:16).

Consequence: Companion of Choice

Choice has a constant companion: consequence. For every action, there is a reaction, a result, an outcome—a *consequence*. One of the constant challenges we face in life is that of anticipating, examining and being influenced by the consequences of our choices. Unfortunately, we can't always see the other side of the decisions we make. God does not give us pre-flight itineraries for our journey through life, nor does divine providence always reveal what's around the corner of the paths we choose.

Yet God makes no secret of how He wants us to choose, as He says in Deuteronomy: "I have set before you life and death, blessing and cursing; therefore choose life" (Deut. 30:19).

To paraphrase Robert Browning, the nineteenth-century poet and playwright, the "business" of life is making an endless series of choices.[2] As we move from one choice to another, the decision we make from each of those choices can dramatically impact the course of our entire life. There is no better example of this truth than how we handle our money.

For example, when handling monetary and financial matters, people often choose to go it alone, refusing to follow God's ways, processes and commands. This is why so many people in today's culture live paycheck to paycheck, struggling just to keep their heads above water. Because they choose not to learn to make their money truly count, they establish a pattern that they follow throughout their lives, without ever realizing that God teaches a far more peaceful and successful way to deal with their finances. His teachings bring prosperity, as He says in Proverbs 3:1-2: "My son, do not forget my teaching, but keep my commands in your heart, for they will prolong your life many years and bring you prosperity" (*NIV*).

In many cases, the contemporary church does not teach God's way of dealing with finances and monetary matters in its entirety. This partial gospel has crept into other areas as well, affecting how we approach such topics as healing and deliverance. For example, we preach and teach healing, yet we say very little about how to *stay* healthy. We preach much about deliverance—conducting deliverance conferences and deliverance services, and walking people through deliverance lines—but we don't say much about how *not* to get into bondage in the first place!

It's the same with monetary affairs. We preach prosperity and financial success, but in most cases we preach and proclaim prosperity without discussing a *process* for achieving that prosperity. There are thousands of people naming it, claiming it and framing it—but if the truth be told, while they may be believing it, most are not receiving it. It's not their fault. It's faulty teaching.

We might not like to admit it, but too often what is taught and preached and proclaimed is a gospel of prosperity that completely ignores the biblical process. This incomplete interpretation of Scripture can easily breed immature, gullible and lazy saints, because they are not being taught the full gospel on the topic. Many Christians don't respond to God's teachings and principles on this subject because they simply haven't been properly taught about it. Then there are those who insist on learning the hard way, even when the Person asking them to trust and follow His ways is Christ Himself.

Too many people are waiting for some kind of supernatural move of God to make them prosperous. They're waiting for wealth to fall like manna from the sky, like silver dollars from heaven—just as soon as their spiritual slot machine lines up right. However, by eliminating *process* from *prosperity*, they've got exactly two chances of getting supernaturally what they're waiting for: slim and none.

God is a God of order, not of chaos. There is an order to how He goes about His work, a process that He always follows.

A Kingdom Principle

It is of grave concern that the Church today paints an incomplete picture of the subject of handling money. Removing God's process from the picture ignores a valuable instructive parable Jesus taught on the topic of financial affairs. What Jesus taught is *God's* process, not man's, and until we not only understand the scope and importance of this teaching but also *put it into practice*, we will continually fall short of our Kingdom potential. We will place ourselves in danger of losing out on God's intended blessings for us and we will render ourselves of little use to Him for His work in the world.

Church folks tend to operate at a sophisticated level of hypocrisy when it comes to money. There are two things they'd like to get more of and hear less about on Sunday, and money is one of them. (Sex is the other.) I realize that the discussion of money might be rather emotional for some readers, but it's time for the saints to stand up and show the world whose children we are: the King who owns it all!

In this book, we will examine what it means to "do business" for Christ's kingdom, and explore the many blessings that await you when you faithfully take care of your financial affairs God's way in an effort to make your money count in today's culture. We will also discover what happens to those who choose much less secure ways to deal with money. As you read, keep in mind that, unless indicated, these aren't merely my own thoughts on the subject. I strain to be faithful to the Word of God as we seek to incorporate into our lives God's own instructions, straight out of His Word.

It's time for believers to put *process* back into prosperity. It's time for us preachers to start teaching the *entire* gospel on the topic of money. It's time for God's children to learn God's process, rather than simply naming and claiming it without fully understanding it.

Ultimately, the choice is yours. You can cling to a partial gospel if you desire, but I guarantee the consequence won't be what you're looking for. On the other hand, if you will learn and wholeheartedly follow *God's ways*, you will achieve great results. It's that simple.

We *can* receive all of the blessings God has in store. We just have to do it His way. So join me and let's explore God's process for achieving financial security and making your money count.

Notes

1. Giovanni Pico della Mirandola (1463–1494), *Oration on the Dignity of Man*, first published in 1486.
2. Robert Browning (1812-1889), *The Ring and the Book*, chapter 10, "The Pope."

SECTION I

The Kingdom Call

You must continue in the things which you have learned and been assured of, knowing from whom you have learned them.

2 TIMOTHY 3:14

God's Word About Money

As followers of God, it is crucial that we learn what He has to say about business and money, and that we then *do* as He instructs.

God's Word contains ample teaching and admonition on the subject. In fact, it is an important enough topic that in the *New King James Version* of the Bible, the words "money" and "riches" appear more than 215 times in all. We won't examine every one of these references, but by the time you're finished reading this book, you will have gained a solid grasp on what God has to say about money and how we are to handle it.

Before we can get right with money, we have to be right with God. This verse illustrates the pattern of relationship between God and man: "And *my* God shall supply all your need according to his riches in glory by Christ Jesus" (Phil. 4:19, emphasis added).

It all starts with those two short words, "my God." Acknowledging and embracing God for who He is, is foundational to learning His precepts concerning money. "My God" presupposes three things:

1. A personal relationship with God
2. Acknowledgment of God as Lord
3. The necessity for salvation (which acknowledgment of God implies)

Once our relationship to God is stated, we move on to the rest of the verse: "shall supply," which illuminates the *nature* of God: He is our supplier. It explains what God shall do for you: "supply all your need," which defines His role as the need-meeter in your life, and your role as the object of His provision.

Then the verse moves on to indicate what His supply for you consists of: "His riches." It sounds like a one-sided relationship, with God doing all the giving and us doing all of the receiving. But remember the condition: We first have to acknowledge Him as our God, humbling ourselves before Him and acknowledging that we are dependent upon Him for *all* of our supply. Once the relationship between God and man is defined, then we can move on to the relationship between man and money.

God supplies for His children. One of the ways He supplies is through instruction in His Word, which we'll look at in the first section of this book. We will also examine some major biblical passages that deal with money, including:

- The parable of the minas, as told by Jesus to His disciples in Luke 19:11–26
- God's five blessings of money
- The purpose of money

- Spiritual maturity
- How the tithe fits in

As we delve into God's Word and explore His teachings on the topic of money, you will begin to see all of the blessings He has in store for you as you commit to follow His process and His ways!

Chapter 1

Prosperity: Just the Facts

I have come that they may have life, and that they may have it more abundantly.

John 10:10

Before we go any further, let's clear up one issue: Poverty vs. Prosperity. Does God want Christians to have wealth or not? Two opposing teachings emanate from church pulpits on this topic today. One narrowly equates material possessions with blessings from God, and the other teaches almost a "deification" of poverty, as if it's a holy virtue to be poor. One camp measures spirituality by the *accumulation* of material possessions, and the other measures it by the *sacrifice* of material possessions.

Are we more spiritual if we have more things or are we more spiritual if we have less? Which teaching is from God? Let's find out. God says:

> Blessed is the man who walks not in the counsel of the ungodly, nor stands in the path of sinners, nor sits in the seat of the scornful; but his delight is in the law of the Lord, and in His law he meditates day and night. He shall be like a tree planted by the rivers of water, that brings forth its fruit in its season, whose leaf also shall not wither; and whatever he does shall prosper (Ps. 1:1-3).

The word "blessed" in this psalm stems from the Hebrew word *esher*, which means "blessings" (plural), indicating a plurality of intensity or magnitude. In other words, happiness is a byproduct of the choices we make, and the person who carefully considers his choices in life increases his chances for happiness.

According to Psalm 1:1-3, the happy person does not walk in the counsel of the ungodly but *chooses* instead to follow the law of the Lord. Acting only on choices that honor God is what leads to happiness and prosperity. The problem comes when people make the mistake of equating material possessions with God's blessings. While it is possible to gain material possessions and financial prosperity as a result of *not* loving and obeying and honoring God, that wealth would not stem from God blessing your actions and has far less of a chance to bring lasting happiness with it. However, there is an even worse downside in attempting to gain prosperity outside of the ways of God: If God is not the source of your material possessions and riches, there's only one other place it could have come from! If you're gaining wealth by following the devil (intentionally or not), he will eventually extract a heavy price from you.

Blessing is manifest by divine favor, a favor that includes both material *and* spiritual blessings. The first time God ever made a pronouncement of blessings on someone was what we refer to as the "Abrahamic Covenant," which He made with Abraham when He said, "I will bless you and make your name great" (Gen. 12:2). God specifically included material blessings in the Abrahamic Covenant—a part of the covenant was the blessing of land and wealth. God says that as we walk in His ways, we will live our life under His hand of divine favor, enjoying the wealth of His material and spiritual blessings.

Biblical Prosperity: An Oxymoron?

Many people ask, "Is prosperity really God's intention for us?" *TIME* magazine posed the question more bluntly in its September 18, 2006, issue with a cover that blared, "Does God Want You to Be Rich?"

Let's break that question down from the bottom up by a process of elimination, followed by what God has to say on the topic. First and foremost, however, you must settle in your mind the definition of "God" and the question of exactly who God is. If you don't believe in the God of the Bible and if you don't believe that the Bible is true, then skip this chapter and we'll catch up with you in the next one.

If you do believe in the God of the Bible and in the inerrancy of Scripture, and you want to know what He has to say on the topic of prosperity and how it relates to Christians, then we can address the first question, which is, Does God want us to be financially destitute? The answer is no, there are no Scriptures to support that premise. However, God does not want us to *want* to be rich simply for the sake of being rich, as it says in 1 Timothy 6:9: "Those who desire to be rich fall into temptation and a snare, and into many foolish and harmful lusts which drown men in destruction and perdition."

The second question is, Does God want us to be monetarily mediocre? Again, there are no Bible verses that support striving for mediocrity. After all, we are children and heirs of the God who owns it all, according to Galatians 4:7: "Therefore you are no longer a slave but a son, and if a son, then an heir of God through Christ."

The third question is, What are God's thoughts on prosperity—does He want us to prosper? Let's take that question directly to God Himself and allow Him to answer from His own Scriptures (emphasis added):

- He who trusts in the LORD *will prosper* (Prov. 28:25, *NIV*).
- Do not turn from it to the right hand or to the left, *that you may prosper* wherever you go (Josh. 1:7).
- Walk in all the way that the LORD your God has commanded you, so that you may live *and prosper* (Deut. 5:33, *NIV*).
- Therefore keep the words of this covenant, and do them, *that you may prosper* in all that you do (Deut. 29:9).

- Keep the charge of the LORD your God: to walk in His ways, to keep His statutes, His commandments, His judgments, and His testimonies, as it is written in the Law of Moses, that *you may prosper* in all that you do (1 Kings 2:3).

- The LORD commanded us to obey all these decrees and to fear the LORD our God, so that we might *always prosper* (Deut. 6:24, *NIV*).

- A generous man *will prosper* (Prov. 11:25, *NIV*).

- He will *prosper you* and multiply you more than your fathers (Deut. 30:5).

- Believe in the LORD your God, and you shall be established; believe His prophets, and *you shall prosper* (2 Chron. 20:20).

I could go on and on with scriptural examples, but that would be like shooting fish in a barrel. However, let's look at one final example, Proverbs 10:22: "The blessing of the LORD makes one rich."

The Hebrew for "blessing" in this verse is *berakah*, which means "abundance." The Hebrew for the word "rich" is *ashar*, which means "accumulation" or "to cause to grow rich." Thus, the transliteration (literal translation) of Proverbs 10:22 is this: "Abundance from God is to give you accumulation to cause you to grow rich." Does that leave any room for doubt about God's intentions toward us with regard to the topic?

But then look at the last part of the verse: "And He adds no sorrow with it." What an astounding little addition to God's stated intention! When God blesses us, we not only accumulate and get rich, but also there is no worry, pain or strife in the process—He wants it to be easy and painless for us! And His only caveat is that we follow *His* ways, trust His leading, His plan, His process and His path (see Lev. 25:18-19). That's it!

There are scores of biblical verses that give us God's clear answer to *TIME* magazine's blaring question, "Does God Want You to be Rich?"—an answer that perhaps *TIME* did not anticipate: If we do as the Bible instructs, if we do as God tells us, if we follow His commands, if we trust His lead . . . then *Yes, He wants us to prosper!* There is no doubt. God makes it very clear.

Distorters of His Word

Do not make the mistake of thinking that this is a prosperity message book. There are Christians who actually believe that it is God's will that every Christian be wealthy and that we're somehow in disobedience to God if we're not financially well off. Those people most likely have dust on their Bibles. There are preachers who shout to their congregations, "It is not God's desire that you suffer financial struggles!"

Well, it might not be God's *desire* that we suffer anything, but sometimes it just might be His will that we do. Here's why: There are times when suffering is the only way some of God's more stubborn children will learn certain lessons. Sometimes I, as a parent, desire that my children suffer a struggle if they're involved in ongoing sin—a struggle may be the only way to get their attention so that they'll stop whatever behavior is causing them to not grow spiritually. What good parent never disciplined their children?

If you've been struggling financially and monetary hardships are a pattern in your life, maybe there are biblical processes governing money that you need to learn and put into practice. The fact is, we have a responsibility to be all that God has called us to be in the area of finances. This means that if God has given you a certain academic preparation, if He has given you a mind to think and to reason with, if He has blessed you with intellect or talents or gifts that can benefit you in being rewarded in financial ways—and yet you don't make the effort to get up and go to class, don't study, don't do your work—you are desecrating what God has given you. You are living beneath that which God has ordained you to live.

God has blessed you with the ability to prosper. That means that on the journey of your life, He has called you to be the man or woman He wants you to be. But if you settle for less, you are dishonoring the God who endowed you with potential for much more. There isn't anything that you cannot reasonably accomplish by doing things the way Jesus teaches. After all, it says in His Word that "I can do all things through Christ who strengthens me" (Phil. 4:13).

To prosper means *to succeed to the point of excellence*—to the highest level. God will bless you with everything you need on your journey to the top of the mountain, and He will help you through every valley until you arrive at the highest point of success He has ordained for you. All you have to do is put His process into play. "'For I know the plans I have for you,' declares the LORD, 'plans to prosper you and not to harm you, plans to give you hope and a future'" (Jer. 29:11, *NIV*).

Prosperity Is a Journey

On the first day of the week let each one of you lay something aside, storing up as he may prosper, that there be no collections when I come.

1 CORINTHIANS 16:2

Beloved, I pray that you may prosper in all things and be in health, just as your soul prospers.

3 JOHN 1:2

Prosperity is an established Old Testament concept. In fact, 27 of 29 occurrences of the word "prosperity" are found in the Old Testament.

The word for "prosper" in the New Testament verses above has a slightly different connotation than the Old Testament word. It indicates *wellbeing on a journey*, moving along on your journey while enjoying wellness and progressive success. The idea is that you do well on your journey through life, in all areas of your life, just as you may be well in your health.

Psalm 1 says that the person who is blessed—who is happy, who does well, who walks in the counsel of the Lord—that person shall prosper. The main Hebrew verb translated into English as "prosper" is *tsalach*, or *tsa-leach*. It means "to push forward, to break out, to come mightily, to go over, to be profitable, to cause to prosper." *Tsalach* is an action word that signifies moving forward, going over, or breaking through. It is meant to convey that the person who is happy and prospering is the one whose life is constantly moving forward. Indeed, they are actually being *pushed* forward—there is something behind them propelling them ahead, compelling them onward.

The idea of prospering is that of a journey. When you are prospering, you are continuing to move forward on your path. To say that you are prospering does not mean that you won't get into a jam, experience challenges or encounter obstacles now and then. Occasional problems will always crop up on our path through life. But we deal with them. We prosper by whatever (or *Whomever*) is propelling us. We are able to go over whatever barrier or hurdle is in our way. We will break out!

True prosperity is simply *success God's way*. The person God prospers is the one whose path is cleared by God because she is following right behind God on His path. The word "prosperity" is related to the word "succeed," which means that God will clear the way and lead you on your journey so that you will arrive at the place He has prepared for you. Once you grasp what true biblical prosperity is and you begin to separate biblical truth from much of this off-kilter contemporary theology on prosperity, you will gain a fresh revelation of how God wants to move through your life—and to make your journey through life *move*!

Let's take a look at a biblical example of prosperity.

Joseph: A Life Journey of Prosperity

The L*ORD* *was with Joseph, and he was a successful man;*
and he was in the house of his master the Egyptian.
And his master saw that the L*ORD* *was with him*
and that the L*ORD* *made all he did to prosper in his hand.*

GENESIS 39:2-3

The Bible says that Joseph was prosperous because the Lord was with him. Joseph was the youngest of 11 brothers. He was a dreamer and an idealist. His brothers considered him a spoiled brat. Being the youngest and having been born when his father, Abraham, was past his golden years, Joseph was the favored child. His father even gave him a special, richly ornamented robe to wear (see Gen. 37:3). His 10 brothers began to grow jealous of him, so they schemed to toss him down a well and be rid of him for once and for all. In a way, their plan backfired. It also set up the entire story of redemption through the incredible history of Israel.

Joseph was sold into slavery to some merchants known as Ishmaelites who took him to Egypt and sold him as a slave to Potiphar, one of Pharaoh's officials and the captain of Pharaoh's palace guard.

Things got better. Joseph, due to his diligence, his obedience to God and no doubt to his perpetually cheery outlook and charming persona, was soon appointed as chief of staff over Potiphar's household.

Things got worse. Joseph was falsely accused by Potiphar's wife of trying to rape her. He was thrown into prison, where he languished for a few years.

Things got better. Eventually, the truth of Joseph's honest character came to light. He was put in a position to assist Pharaoh in an urgent matter, and he was appointed as one of the highest officials in all of Egypt, second in authority only to Pharaoh himself.

Joseph did not wait until he became the minister of the treasury of Egypt before he began to prosper. In fact, he was prospering every step of the way, from back when he ran Potiphar's household. *Joseph prospered.* Even when he was in jail, Joseph was prospering!

Joseph prospered because his ultimate position of leadership in Egypt was God's purpose for him. He achieved that purpose because he trusted God and followed Him every step of the way. All those steps along the way—being sold by his brothers into slavery, serving in Potiphar's house, being wrongfully locked up in jail, being released by Pharaoh who then appointed him second in command over the most powerful nation on Earth—were all steps in his prosperity journey process.

Joseph was on a journey toward the blessed responsibility of leading an entire nation in good times and in bad. Nothing he experienced and suffered and conquered was haphazard—every step of the way was ordained by God. Sometimes his path led through trying circumstances, because in order for God to get Joseph all the way to his destiny, He had to take him over some rough roads. But He brought Joseph through. And Joseph never shirked his path: He embraced it, submitted to it, sought it. Indeed, he followed God's path for his life with a positive outlook and with never a recorded complaint. Joseph was mightily blessed and prospered because of his attitude and his obedience.

Joseph is an example of prosperity because his journey to the pinnacle of responsibility over Egypt was his purpose, and everything that led him to that point was a crucial steppingstone to his prosperity, a rung on his ladder to the top. It was all part of the weave of God's pattern for the life of Joseph. Likewise, your prosperity is inextricably woven into the fabric of your life's purpose. God allows you to experience the highs and lows of life because prosperity is integrated within your purpose as you move along your journey.

The Unstudied Naysayers

Too many people don't study the Scriptures in-depth enough to realize one simple fact: The Bible *never* contradicts itself. It *is* definitive on the topic of money, prosperity, finances and income. The Christian naysayers, the detractors, who claim that a person cannot be Christian and also be prosperous or rich simply don't study their Bible closely enough.

In explaining their position, those of the poverty mind-set often point to verses such as this one, from the book of Matthew:

> Do not lay up for yourselves treasures on earth, where moth and rust destroy and where thieves break in and steal; but lay up for yourselves treasures in Heaven, where neither moth nor rust destroys and where thieves do not break in and steal. For where your treasure is, there your heart will be also (Matt. 6:19-21).

People who use this passage in support of their mission to prove that God doesn't want us to be wealthy, miss one key word in the passage: *yourselves*. "Do not lay up for *yourselves* . . ." Of course we're not supposed to lay up material blessings for ourselves—the Bible clearly teaches that we're not to hoard it, but that we're to share it once we get it.

These same people also quote selections from the Old Testament to try to prove that Christians should not seek to prosper:

> Do not be afraid when one becomes rich, when the glory of his house is increased; for when he dies he shall carry nothing away; his glory shall not descend after him. Though while he lives he blesses himself (for men will praise you when you do

> well for yourself), he shall go to the generation of his fathers; they shall never see light. A man who is in honor, yet does not understand, is like the beasts that perish (Ps. 49:16-20).

People who use these verses to prove their anti-prosperity argument also miss one simple phrase: "the glory of *his* house is increased." Of course we're not to seek the glory of *our* house, but the glory of *God's* house. Then there's the phrase in the same passage, "while he lives *he blesses himself*." Again, the Bible is clear: We are not to use our material possessions, our prosperity, merely to bless ourselves, but *to bless others*, to do *God's* work, to advance *His* Kingdom on Earth.

A passage in James is also often used against prosperity:

> Come now, you rich, weep and howl for your miseries that are coming upon you! Your riches are corrupted, and your garments are moth-eaten. Your gold and silver are corroded, and their corrosion will be a witness against you and will eat your flesh like fire. You have heaped up treasure in the last days (Jas. 5:1-3).

Again, the obvious is missed right in the very verse they use to state their case. The clarification is in the verse itself: "*your* riches" (referring to a wealthy person whose mind-set is that their riches are their own). Any Christian who studies the Bible on the topic knows that riches are not ours; they're God's. The verse is indicating people who think that riches are their own property to do with as they please—it is *not* indicating that Christians should not have stewardship over riches.

Then, in the same passage, there's the phrase "you have heaped up." This refers to *hoarding for oneself*, again indicating a mind-set of possessing for one's own benefit.

I could go on and on about these faulty teachers' lack of study and their preaching a partial gospel on the subject, using the very Bible verses they quote in alleged support of their claim that God doesn't want Christians to become prosperous or wealthy. Scripture is crystal clear on the subject: When we treat treasures as ours, when we start to think of material blessings as our own personal property to do with as we please, then we've gone off track. It's *never* ours—it is always God's, entrusted to us for but a season. And if we deliberately mess up, God will discipline us, just as He promises, "You rebuke and discipline men for their sin; you consume their wealth like a moth" (Ps. 39:11, *NIV*).

But Is It of God?

Anything that looks like prosperity but does not enhance your purpose is not of God! If it does not bring glory to God, if it does not illuminate your Christian walk, if it does not represent the character of Jesus Christ, then I don't care how good it looks, how great it feels, how big it is—it is a deception and an indication that you have been walking in the counsel of the ungodly. You will become prosperous only to the degree that you are moving toward the things of God, because with God, it is not about money. Neither God nor the devil is upset when you gain material wealth. The enemy is only concerned with giving you whatever it takes to keep you away from your destiny in God, and God is only concerned that you follow His purpose for your life, that you follow His Holy Spirit, His ways, His processes.

Prosperity is contextually relevant to our purpose. In other words, we prosper in the environment of our purpose, because prosperity is part of the fulfillment of the specific call of God on our lives. Therefore, godly prosperity is deemed to be so *only* if it advances us on our journey to our destiny with God in this world. It does not matter how attractive the "stuff" looks on the side of the road, because as soon as you turn off the path and go after what you think looks good but is not from God, it pulls you away from your purpose and your destiny.

Something may *look* prosperous to you, but if it is not part of your journey with God, it has distracted you from your destiny and purpose, and God says it is not from Him. And if it's not from God, the process of elimination tells you who such distractions are from.

That brings us to the potential trip-up: If he has to, the devil will resort to trying to *bless* you out of your purpose! He will try to distract you so that you get off the course of your prosperity journey. Many people fall for that, so Jesus has to come along and remind them: "What will it profit a man if he gains the whole world, and loses his own soul?" (Mark 8:36).

The devil is not concerned about your getting rich or having money. The devil wants you to miss your purpose. The devil wants you off of God's track for your life, and that's all he wants, because he knows something that he does not want us to ever realize: It is possible to gain the whole world *and* gain your soul as well! Just follow the precepts, the processes, the ways of God, and like Joseph you'll prosper on Earth and enter victorious into heaven at your appointed time.

By Our Fruit

The Bible says, "by their fruits ye shall know them" (Matt. 7:20, *KJV*). That is, we Christians shall be known by our "fruit"—by what we do, how we treat people, how and if we help those in need. If we have no fruit, how shall they know us? If we have no ability to help, to assist, to step in during the hard times when suffering people are in need, how will we be known?

Many pastors don't enjoy preaching about money, material blessings and prosperity, simply because they have not studied Scripture in depth enough to gain acuity on the subject. There are even preachers who blatantly discourage their flocks from thinking that God looks favorably on prosperity. But what do we do with Joseph? What do we do with King David? What do we do with Moses and Matthew and Zacchaeus and Joseph of Arimathea and on and on and on? Does their wealth condemn them? Of course not. In fact, wealth was often an essential component to serving God and operating in their God-ordained purpose. Without money, for example, Joseph of Arimathea couldn't have purchased the private tomb for Jesus.

Then there are the so-called ministers of prosperity who essentially say that the way to help the poor is to *encourage them not to be poor*. Encouraging someone without helping them does nothing for the poor. You help the poor by *helping* them. Platitudes don't help a needy person pay her rent, and it's much easier to help pay her rent when you have the financial means to do so. You gain the means by obeying the Word of God and by allowing His process to work in your life as you follow His purpose for you. If God wants you to be rich in order to fulfill His purpose through you, then who are you to say, "Oh, no thank you, Lord—my pastor told me wealth is wrong for us Christians. But thanks anyway"?

I don't know one single Christian who honestly believes that Jesus died the most violent death possible and then rose from the grave to glory in heaven just so that we could be "blessed" to live a life full of mediocrity and failure and poverty and financial struggle. Do we honestly think our Father in heaven prefers that for us? What kind of a father would want that for his children? It's time to snap out of that way of thinking. If you're a parent, answer this question honestly: Would you prefer that your children and grandchildren be constantly preoccupied with a struggle to make ends meet, or would you rather they not have that worry on their minds?

I have found an interesting contradiction: Some of the very same people who espouse a theology of anti-wealth and anti-possessions are involved in ministries that are supported by Christian millionaires!

A millionaire who funds a mission and a ministry is accountable for gaining as much money as possible and then turning around to channel those funds back into the ministry–it behooves that person to be as rich and as wealthy as God would have him be. God gave him the power to get it so that he could then give it, so that He can reestablish His covenant and pour it back into the Kingdom. All the while, God gets the glory and many people get blessed along the way. That process, as Ecclesiastes says, is a gift from God!

> It is good and fitting for one to eat and drink, and to enjoy the good of all his labor in which he toils under the sun all the days of his life which God gives him; for it is his heritage. As for every man to whom God has given riches and wealth, and given him power to eat of it, to receive his heritage and rejoice in his labor–this is the gift of God (Eccles. 5:18-19).

Don't fall for the two extremes that have crept into the Church today. Don't believe on one hand that God's blessings are all about money, but don't believe on the other that God's blessings are never about money. God's blessings and His purpose for you are above and beyond anything that you can imagine. His blessings include spiritual richness, and they also encompass monetary wealth.

In the Joy of Joseph

God's ultimate goal for your life is that you gain all of the worldly "stuff" that He has purposed you to have *and* have your soul as well. You have a responsibility to be as rich as God would have you to be. You have a responsibility to live up to your purpose. You are accountable to be as blessed and as wealthy as your purpose in God dictates.

I have a strong desire to one day live on 10 percent of what I make and to be able to give 90 percent back into the kingdom of God on

Earth. I'm not saying I'm so noble or deep or spiritual. I'm just saying that's what the Holy Spirit is urging within me.

Do you know how much I need to earn in order to be able to afford to live on 10 and give 90? Is that even possible? With God it is! I will have to break away from some distractions and nonproductive influences, but it will be worth it because I guarantee that the 10 I'll live on then will be better than the 90 I'm living on now!

What do you want for your life? Are you willing to give glory to God's name in order to receive His glory on your purpose? Whatever purpose God is calling you to, live it fully. Don't reject any of it! Embrace it joyfully, as Joseph always did. God says that the person who is happy will prosper. Once you get the *definition* of prosperity, God will give you the *directions* for prosperity.

Psalm 1:3 says that whatever the obedient person does shall prosper. Why? Because his delight is in the law of the Lord! Start living your life in the delight of God's law, and watch your life prosper!

I echo the apostle John's prayer for you: *I pray that you may prosper in all things and be in health, just as your soul prospers!*

CHAPTER 2

Message of the Minas

He spoke another parable, because He was near Jerusalem
and because they thought the kingdom of God would appear immediately.
Therefore He said: "A certain nobleman went into a far country
to receive for himself a kingdom and to return.
So he called ten of his servants, delivered to them ten minas,
and said to them, 'Do business till I come.'"

LUKE 19:11-13

The parable of the minas is one of the most powerful passages in Scripture for helping us to understand God's instructions about money. A mina is a weight of coin that today would be worth between $15 and $20. The *King James Version* calls them pounds. *The Living Bible* translation says the nobleman "gave them each $2,000 to invest while he was gone." *THE MESSAGE* simply says it was "a sum of money." Whatever the amount, this parable clearly reveals God's process governing what we are to do with money and how to oversee our financial affairs in ways that reveal to Him that we can be trusted with His resources.

It is no accident that Jesus speaks this parable when He does, right after dining with a man named Zacchaeus. In verse 2 of Luke 19, we meet Zacchaeus and we learn two things about him: He is a tax collector and he is rich. It is likely that these facts were the impetus for Jesus' teaching of this parable. One thing that surely prompted the teaching was the faulty expectation of Jesus' disciples that Christ's kingdom had finally come on Earth and that His reign was going to be established immediately.

> He was near Jerusalem and . . . they thought the kingdom of God would appear immediately (Luke 19:11).

The disciples also assumed that the arrival of *Mashiyach* (Messiah) meant that they would no longer have to work and defend and slave and toil. They took for granted that since Jesus had finally arrived on the scene as foretold in the Torah, He surely was about to vanquish the oppressive Roman rule and set up His kingdom on Earth.

"Not so fast," Jesus says, in effect. "There is much to be done before all that takes place." And so He told them this instructive parable, which did three things:

1. It *foreshadowed* His departure via crucifixion.
2. It *informed* the disciples that they still had a duty to perform in His absence.
3. It *instructed* them that their job was to conduct business until He returned.

The underlying message was that Jesus would be going away soon to be given His kingdom by God, and that while He was about His business, the disciples were also to be about business. Since *we* too are disciples of Jesus, the lesson applies to us: We are to be about business, with the resources God has given us, until Christ returns.

But what does that mean, exactly?

Work It

The parable says that when the king called 10 of his servants together, he gave them each a mina. In that time and economy, a mina was the equivalent of approximately three months' wages. Along with the mina,

He gave them a command. It was not a suggestion or a mere instruction—it was a *command*. The phrase in Greek means *to do the activity of a trader or a banker*. The tense of the phrase "till I come" means to do business *while I am coming*. In other words, "I am coming, and while I'm coming, there's something you need to do." That "something," Jesus is saying, is *doing business*.

So here we have Jesus giving the disciples instructions to perform a task that at first glance doesn't appear all that spiritual. This is significant. Everything we do is within our spiritual relationship to God, but not all we do is necessarily spiritual in nature. In other words, we must still live in, dwell in and be a part of this world. There is no separation for us between the sacred and the secular—it's all lumped into *life*. And here God gives us an instructive example of something that takes place within the frame of the world system. It is pragmatic. It is practical. It is down to earth. It is mundane. It's *business*.

Let's look again at the command itself. Wrapped up in the command to do business (or "to occupy") is the concept of performing the activity of a trader or a banker. In other words, the master is saying, "Invest my money—put it to work until I come back." He did not say give it away. He did not say bury it and keep it safe. He said *do business with it*! Trade with it. Make an increase of this money.

He left each servant with a portion of money, along with brief instructions. And after a while, he returned . . .

> And so it was that when he returned, having received the kingdom, he then commanded these servants, to whom he had given the money, to be called to him, that he might know how much every man had gained by trading. Then came the first, saying, "Master, your mina has earned ten minas." And he said to him, "Well done, good servant; because you were faithful in a very

> little, have authority over ten cities." And the second came, saying, "Master, your mina has earned five minas." Likewise he said to him, "You also be over five cities" (Luke 19:15-19).

When the master came back, each servant gave him a report. One man said, "Master, your mina has earned ten minas." That's a tenfold increase–one thousand percent of what he started with–not bad at all. He began with one and now has ten. The master responded, "Well done, faithful servant. I will give you authority over ten cities." Watch the progression as it is linked to the reward: The first servant received an amount of money, and in reward for increasing it from one to ten, he received ten cities to rule over.

The next fellow came and said, "Master, your mina has gained five." Notice the same progression. "Well done," the Master said. "I'll give you authority over five cities." Again, gain was made and a reward given.

Through the activity of conducting business, they gained many from just one. How did the men gain ten and five from just one? The answer is in the text. They *put the money to work*! They did business.

The word "business" is from the Greek word *pragmateuomai*, which is the root for our words "pragmatism" and "pragmatic." The word "gain" is a derivative of the same word, *pragmateuomai*. The parallel Hebrew term for "doing business" is *asah mela'kah,* which means "to dispatch as a deputy; a messenger, specifically of God; ambassador; i.e., ministry; employment or work."[1] The Hebrew term also refers to property gained as the result of labor, business, cattle, industry, occupation or workmanship.

In short, they did business and the money gained. "Doing business" is presented in this parable as a very practical, pragmatic, normal endeavor.

Here's how the various Bible translations present the phrase "do business":

KJV:	"Occupy till I come."
NKJV:	"Do business till I come."
NIV:	"Put this money to work . . . until I come back."
NRSV:	"Do business with these until I come back."
NASB:	"Do business with this until I come back."
THE MESSAGE:	"Operate with this until I return."
AMP:	"Buy and sell with these while I go and then return."
NLT:	"Invest for him while he was gone."
ESV:	"Engage in business until I come."
CEB:	"Use this to earn more money until I get back."
ASV:	"Trade ye herewith till I come."
TLB:	"Invest while he was gone."

The message is the same, no matter which version you use. Many people attempt to spiritualize the Luke 19 passage and make it about something it's not. The fact is, Jesus was teaching a sensible, down-to-earth *pragmateuomai* truth about money. No matter how you slice it, no matter what translation you read the story in, it's clear that Jesus was talking about practicalities. The nobleman said, "Take the money; and while I'm away, do business with it. Buy and sell, perform the activity of a trader, banker or businessperson."

Remember, not everything we do as Christians will necessarily be a "spiritual" undertaking, but it will still remain within the context of our spiritual relationship with God—it will be sanctified when we do it in His name and in His way.

The Third Man

Parables contain symbolism. In this parable, the nobleman—the master—symbolizes Jesus Himself. The servants symbolize us, God's people, followers of the King.

When he was preparing to leave, the nobleman called 10 of his servants and gave to each of them one mina and a simple instruction: *Take this money and do business with it until I return*. When the nobleman gave his money over to his servants' trust, three components were put into play:

1. He gave the servants explicit instructions as to what he wanted them to do with his money: *Do business*.

2. There was an unspoken expectation delivered with his explicit instructions: *Gain more money* (and certainly don't lose it).

3. There will be a final accounting: *Until I return* (which brought with it the insinuation of judgment or reward, depending on the results).

The first component was explicit. The second was implied. The third went unspoken. None of the servants were given any warning that if they didn't make at least a sensible effort with the master's money, there would be dire consequences. However, God has graciously given *us* such a warning—through this very parable.

The master was a businessman who earned some of his money by having others invest it on his behalf. He expected his servants to behave the same way with his money, or to at least give it a good faith effort. When the master returned from doing his business, he called each of his servants before him to inquire how they had fared in conducting their business. He wanted to know how much each had gained by trading with his money. Note that each servant started with the same amount, one mina. One servant turned his one mina into 10. Another man turned his one mina into five. Both men were rewarded greatly, with the one who gained 10 receiving authority over 10 cities, and the one who gained five receiving authority over five cities.

Then we arrive at the third man . . . and the lesson hits the flipside.

The third man came before the master and delivered a very interesting report: "Master, here is your mina, which I have kept put away in a handkerchief. For I feared you, because you are an austere man. You collect what you did not deposit, and reap what you did not sow" (Luke 19:20-21).

The third man kept the master's money in a handkerchief! This servant, who started with one mina just like the other guys, did nothing with his mina but bury it contemptuously in the ground. How uncreative can you get? He didn't even deposit it in the bank so that his master could have at least earned a little interest on his money.

The third man, by doing nothing with the master's mina, set himself up for strict judgment. He said to his master, "I kept it in a handkerchief"—as if that might help a little, maybe keep the mina shiny. But he may as well have just told his master, "I didn't do what you asked me to do with your money in your absence, boss. Heck, I didn't even *try* to earn any profit or even *attempt* to do any business with it. I didn't make any effort whatsoever. Matter of fact, chief, I stashed it in a hanky and stuck it in the ground. Sure, I heard your instructions—I'm not deaf. But man, you're *hard*! I didn't want to take a chance of ticking you off in case I failed to earn you a profit. So, I thought it might be best if I just . . . did nothing at all."

I'll bet the people gathered there cringed when he told the master he did nothing with the money. You could probably hear the master's jaw drop as that third servant announced, "Master, I buried it in the ground." The guy practically went out of his way to make sure the mina wouldn't even earn one mite's worth of interest. Didn't express remorse that what he did went completely counter to his master's orders. Didn't seem to think there was anything particularly wrong with what he did. He merely explained his disobedience in a very matter-of-fact way, as if burying money in a hanky in a dirt hole was a normal thing to do.

This third man was laboring under two serious misunderstandings: first, that he could do what he thought best with the money, in direct disobedience to the master's wishes (whose money it was in the first place!); and second, that the money was something to be possessed, hoarded, hidden in the ground and not to be risked, rather than an asset with the potential to gain and grow.

If you think the third man's reaction to his master's instructions was stunning, wait until you see the master's reaction to the servant's impudence:

> He said to him, "Out of your own mouth I will judge you, you wicked servant. You knew that I was an austere man, collecting what I did not deposit and reaping what I did not sow. Why then [since you knew that about me] did you not put my money in the bank, that at my coming I might have collected it with interest?" And he said to those who stood by, "Take the mina from him, and give it to him who has ten minas." (But they said to him, "Master, he has ten minas.") "For I say to you, that to everyone who has will be given; and from him who does not have, even what he has will be taken away from him" (Luke 19:22-26).

Some people might think this punishment was steep, but how did the third man expect his master to respond? It's understandable why the master was so unhappy with the third servant—he didn't even *try* to follow instructions. The master's reaction wasn't even really that harsh, if you think about it. Would he have instructed his men to do something they weren't equipped to at least attempt? The first two servants proved that they had the wherewithal to perform as required—and with outstanding results. The third servant's punishment was pretty light, considering that he flatly refused to do what his master ordered. His disobedience could have cost him much more than merely taking away what he was entrusted with.

Here's how the equations break down:

Equation of the Third Man

He came to the arrangement with nothing:	0
He was given something:	+1
He did nothing with it—he gained nothing:	0
What had been given to him was taken:	-1
He walked away with nothing:	= 0 (+shame)

Equation of the Obedient Servants

They came into the arrangement with nothing:	0
They were given something:	+1
They did something with it and gained:	+4 and +9
They were rewarded for their gain:	= 5 and 10 (entire kingdoms!)

The first two servants did only what was asked of them—*and they walked away with kingdoms at their beck and call.* And they didn't even have to risk their own money. Sweet!

It was all about attitude. The third man's attitude was *nothing ventured, nothing lost*—completely leaving out a factor called *obedience*. The attitude of the other two servants was *nothing ventured, nothing gained*—the attitude of obedient winners.

The third man gives us a clue as to why he ended up with the same measly mina that he started with. He says in Luke 19:20-21, "Master, here is your mina, which I have kept put away in a handkerchief. For I feared you." He was *afraid* of his master!

A Spirit of Fear

What happened to that third man? What threw him so far off course that he disobeyed his master, lost what was given to him and was barred from ruling over a kingdom? *Fear.* Remember, the master didn't merely *suggest* that his servants do business—he *commanded it*. But by acting out of fear—or *not acting* because of fear—the third man walked away from blessings, honor and great reward.

Fear drove him to disobey.

Fear brought him loss.

Fear rendered him a man of shame and scorn.

Fear may have even ruined his entire life, if he didn't learn from the experience.

It's interesting how bits and pieces of biblical truth get carried over into different cultures. My grandmother used to keep her money in a handkerchief. Grandmamma never seemed to care too much about her purse—if somebody took her purse, they'd be in a world of disappointment. In order to get Grandmamma's money, you had to lay hands on her. I think it's a requirement of all grandmothers to have a safe place to stash their cash. It's a Grandma Rule: *Put your money in a safe place somewhere on your person*. Mine wrapped hers in a little handkerchief, and when I needed to buy something, she'd say, "Wait a minute, baby" and turn her back to rummage around somewhere in her clothes. "Wait just a minute, sugar. I'll be right there." She hid her spending money to keep it safe and at hand.

The third servant, on the other hand, hid the money out of rank fear. His master may have been tough, but there is no indication in the text that the master had previously displayed a pattern of cruelty or anger or violence with any of his servants. In fact, none of the other servants expressed any fear of him at all—indeed, he seemed to display a very generous nature.

Fear is one of the central reasons many people do not handle their money correctly. It doesn't matter what economic level you're on—fear can be a problem whether you make $5,000 a year, $50,000 a year or $500,000 a year. Many people fear that they'll lose what they have, so instead of investing it, they hold on to it once they get it. That's exactly what the third man did. He sat on it. The man had only one mina—but so did everyone else. Instead of moving in faith and investing it, he held on to it out of fear that he might lose it. He was afraid. Afraid to invest. Afraid to obey. Afraid to try. Maybe he hadn't been taught, or maybe he didn't pay attention when he was taught, or perhaps he just didn't understand how to handle money. Despite all those possible excuses, he was even afraid to speak up at the time the master gave them their instructions.

God has not given us a spirit of fear, but of power and of love and of a sound mind (see 2 Tim. 1:7). A "sound mind" refers to discipline. The phrase comes from the Greek word *sophronismos*, which has to do with self-control, moderation and discipline. Reject fear. Step off the boat in obedience and faith: *God won't let you drown.* Besides, it's *easy* to follow and work and understand God's process for financial prosperity! Why? Because:

The Money Does the Work!

Then came the first, saying, "Master, your mina has earned . . ."
And the second came, saying, "Master, your mina has earned . . ."

LUKE 19:16,18, EMPHASIS ADDED

I would venture a guess that only 1 percent of the population of America (those that are the most financially secure) have learned something that the other 99 percent have not. That lesson is spelled out right in the Luke 19 text, and it will change your life.

Does the text say "Master, I have gained ten minas"? No. Verses 16 and 18 say, "*your mina has earned.*" It's the mina, the pound, the *money itself* that does the earning! Keep in mind the connection between the subject and the verb:

your = antecedent
money = subject
gained = verb

The verb indicates the action of the subject. In this case, the money is the subject and the action is that *it earned.* The antecedent (that which precedes the subject) is *not* the servant; it's the owner of the money. Hence, *the master's money did the gaining.*

The principal is this: It was not the man who received the gain as much as it was the *money* that received the gain. *The money made more money.* The first two servants knew this, which is why they said to the master, "Your money has earned . . ."

Prosperity is the difference between the haves and the have-nots. The difference between haves and have-nots (the 1 percent of this country and the other 99 percent) is that the 1 percent has learned the secret to making money work for them. Most people are have-nots because only 1 percent of us have learned that you don't work to make money; *you make money work*. The difference between the first two men and the third man is that the first two operated from this Kingdom principle.

Most of us go to school for years to learn skills to get a job to make money, but very few people learn how to make money do a job. Most people go to school to learn how to work in an industry that will pay them money, but very few go to school to learn how to make their money earn money.

Don't get me wrong. I believe in education. I'm a teacher, I'm an educator, I'm a scholar, I'm a student. I've been in school all my life and have four earned degrees to my name (a bachelor's, a master's, a Ph.D. and a Doctorate of Ministry). The church I pastor gives out scholarships. I've put two of my own kids through college and have another one coming along very well. I do believe in education, but we've got to understand that we're living in a world system that is structured to perpetuate—even to *expect*—mediocrity. It is a system geared to keep the great majority of people out of participation in the benefits that come with exercising wise financial stewardship.

We must start learning the biblical concept of making money work for us, not merely how to work for money.

It's a Kingdom Principle

There are Christians who claim they don't care about money. I won't even take the time to deal with them. (Check with them on the first and the fifteenth of each month and see if they still don't care.) I *will* address the myth some have accepted that you have to work harder to earn more money. News flash: You can work harder and still have money problems!

The goal is not to work more to make more money—the goal is to *make money work* so that you can be freed up to do what God has called you to do in His kingdom on Earth. To "do business" means *to invest.* Instead of working for money, we need to make money work for us by investing it. Working harder is not what solves money problems. Even a better education won't guarantee financial stability. That isn't to say those things aren't important, but the most important thing is not how you earn your money but what you do with it.

This is a Kingdom principle. It is not a whim or a theory. The same Bible that proclaims salvation also lays out the principle that money is to earn money. As a biblical teaching, we can be confident of this principle because its Author is God Himself, the Source of all wealth.

Note

1. James Strong, *Strong's Hebrew Lexicon* (Nashville, TN: Thomas Nelson Publishers, 1984), Hebrew no. 4397 (*mela'kah*).

Chapter 3

The Source of All Wealth

Every beast of the forest is Mine, and the cattle on a thousand hills.
I know all the birds of the mountains, and the wild beasts of the field are Mine.
If I were hungry, I would not tell you;
for the world is Mine, and all its fullness.

Psalm 50:10-12

Do you ever stop to think about the words you use? A lot of times we throw words around without really thinking about what they mean. Let's look at one word in particular: "wealth."

"Wealth" is not just another word for "money" or for "riches." Wealth is when more than just our needs are met, when there is an abundance of supplies over and above our needs. It's when we have more money left over at the end of the month instead of more month left at the end of our money.

Wealth is God's ideal plan for us. And it is attainable if we will follow His plan.

Sustainability

The ability to survive so many numbers of days into the future without a steady income is what defines true wealth. For example, the main building of our church, Faithful Central Bible Church, is the Great Western Forum (former home of the L.A. Lakers basketball team). The Forum was built from an architectural design called the geodesic dome. This structural design was patented in 1954 by a man named Buckminster Fuller, who became a multimillionaire off of this patent. He was able to live for the rest of his life without having to work for a living, simply from the fees generated by builders who employed the techniques of his patent.

Fuller's ability to live the rest of his life off of the income generated from his patent is "sustainability"—it is *wealth.* Or take someone such as country singer Garth Brooks, a highly successful musician. I doubt if his future grandchildren will be able to spend all of his money. Or superstar basketball player Michael Jordan. I recall reading a news article when he retired that stated that he never had to work another day in his life.

How long could you survive if you stopped working right now? Have you enslaved yourself to a system that requires you to keep working, or else? How far could you go? How many paychecks could you miss before it starts to hurt? Wealth is the ability to sustain and survive. More specifically, it is the capability to keep paying your bills without having to go to work to earn an income. If you're not in a position right now to quit work and sustain yourself for the rest of your life, it is possible to get to that point!

Based on examples like Michael Jordan or Garth Brooks, you might think you can't have wealth unless you're earning millions of dollars, but that is not necessarily true. Wealth is not created from paychecks—it's created from *assets.* If you look at the salary of most wealthy people, you'd be surprised. Most rich people don't have big incomes, they just know how to make the money they have work for them. Their money is not in their paycheck; it's in their investments. They have learned how to make their assets work for them, how to make their money earn more money. They know the difference between assets and income, and they let their assets earn the income. You can do the same.

Remember, it's not about how much money you earn at work; it's about how much work your money does for you! That is a theme I want you to thoroughly absorb during the course of this study.

To Whom It All Belongs

Wealth speaks of that which has intrinsic value. To truly appreciate wealth, you have to realize its source. That source is God: "'The silver is Mine, and the gold is Mine,' says the LORD of hosts" (Hag. 2:8).

The Scripture above, the one at the beginning of this chapter (Ps. 50:10-12) and many other verses in the Bible speak of God as the owner of everything of value. Silver. Gold. Wild beasts of forest and field. Livestock. The cattle on a thousand hills. Everything of value—He owns it all. God ultimately controls and allocates all wealth. Psalm 50:12 sums it up when God says, "the world is Mine, and all its fullness."

And then there is this tantalizing statement from God, "You shall remember the LORD your God, for it is He who gives you power to get wealth" (Deut. 8:18). Not only does God create what has value, but He also equips His children for attaining it! Scripture does not say "God is *one of those* who gives you power to get wealth." It does not say, "*One source* of getting the power to gain wealth is God" or "God is *one way* to get wealth." The Bible says *it is He*. Many Christians forget this. When they earn or receive money, they think it's their own because they earned it by their work. But it is God who allowed them to obtain that money. God alone. He is the source—both of the wealth itself and of our ability to attain it.

You don't get training at The Boeing Company to learn how to construct a slingshot. You don't go to a coal miner to find out the basics of tap dancing. You don't call a painter to learn about surgery. And you don't sit down with a two-year-old to get training in quantum physics—

whatever that is! If you want to learn about wealth and the power to create or attain it, you go to the Source: God.

So, let's go to the Source and find out what He has to say about wealth.

CHAPTER 4

God's Heart: To Bless His Children

In the parable of the minas (see Luke 19), the master gave the servants that which was to be multiplied. He told them, "Take this and invest it for me while I'm away." It was not to be given away, it was not to be eaten, it was not to be spent, and it was not to be shared with their friends. It was to be *multiplied.* In other words, *take this amount and bring me a profit with it.* Don't stash it in a safe deposit box. Don't bury it in your backyard. Don't put it under your mattress. *Multiply it.* Why? To expand God's kingdom in the world.

Expanding God's kingdom in the world expands His influence in the world. Expanding God's influence in the world increases His visibility in the world. Increasing God's visibility in the world gives more opportunity to bless other people in the world. And blessing other people in the world draws them—and us—closer to God's heart.

To bring all of that about, God has put into place a system, a process.

The passage below reveals God's strikingly uncomplicated model of commerce. It portrays God as both the Supplier and Multiplier of the abundance and as the Recipient of the glory. It portrays God's followers as both the recipients and distributors of the abundance and as administrators of the service. Notice how one component leads to, and builds upon, the next:

> God is able to make all grace abound toward you, [so] that you, always having all sufficiency in all things, may have an abundance for every good work. [So that] He who supplies seed to

> the sower, and bread for food, [may also] supply and multiply the seed you have sown and increase the fruits of your righteousness, [which will occur] while you are [being] enriched in everything for all liberality, which causes thanksgiving [through whom to Whom?] through us to God. For the administration of this service not only supplies the needs of the saints, but also is abounding through many thanksgivings to God (2 Cor. 9:8,10-12).

God's Five Blessings of Money

The passage above reveals five God-ordained blessings of money—that is, how He uses money to bless His children: (1) as seed for the sower; (2) to provide bread; (3) to multiply the seed that is sown; (4) to increase the fruits of our righteousness; and (5) to give. Let's break these down.

Blessing 1: Seed for the Sower

"Seed" can have several different meanings:

- *Children:* Children are "the seed" through which the family line is continued. Through children, the family expands and grows. An example is found in the story of Abraham and the promise God gave to him: "And I will make your descendants multiply as the stars of Heaven; I will give to your descendants all these lands; and in your *seed* all the nations of the earth shall be blessed" (Gen. 26:4).

- *The Word of God:* The Word of God is "seed" in the sense that it causes spiritual growth in the hearts of those who hear and receive it. Luke 8:11 says, "Now the parable is this: The *seed* is the word of God" (emphasis added).

- *Money:* In this context, the seed is that which God gives to us within the economy of the present-day culture. It is the medium of exchange in our society. This is the meaning found in 2 Corinthians 9:10 when Paul writes about "*seed* to the sower both to minister bread for your food, and multiply your seed sown" (*KJV*, emphasis added).

Blessing 2: To Provide Bread

The following passage demonstrates the depth of God's caring love toward us via His ceaseless provision:

> Do not worry about your life, what you will eat or what you will drink; nor about your body, what you will put on. Is not life more than food and the body more than clothing? Look at the birds of the air, for they neither sow nor reap nor gather into barns; yet your Heavenly Father feeds them. Are you not of more value than they? Which of you by worrying can add one cubit to his stature?
>
> So why do you worry about clothing? Consider the lilies of the field, how they grow: they neither toil nor spin; and yet I say to you that even Solomon in all his glory was not arrayed like one of these. Now if God so clothes the grass of the field, which today is, and tomorrow is thrown into the oven, will He not much more clothe you, O you of little faith?
>
> Therefore do not worry, saying, "What shall we eat?" or "What shall we drink?" or "What shall we wear?" For after all these things the Gentiles seek. For your heavenly Father knows that you need all these things (Matt. 6:25-32).

In the homily above, Jesus is telling us, "Don't trip. Don't be anxious, don't consider, don't be upset, don't worry about how you're going to make it tomorrow. Don't trip out on it." As an example of God's provision and love, He says, "Look around. Look at these flowers. Look at these lilies in the fields—nothing in God's creation is arrayed more splendidly than they are." He provides even for the lilies of the fields. He says, "See that little sparrow up there? See that fowl in the air? They don't sow, they don't reap, they don't trip—and yet God provides for them."

We hear a lot in churches these days about *mountain-moving faith*. "Speak to the mountain, 'Mountain, move!'" There are a lot of people out there speaking to mountains that aren't *ever* going to move. Mountain-moving faith is great, but sometimes God is simply not going to move some mountains for us. Why? Because He wants to give us the strength, the ability, the experience to *climb* some of those mountains. At other times, He wants to teach us patience to wait for Him to move the mountains in His good timing. Or He might want to teach us to go through, under or over some mountains ourselves.

Mountain-moving faith implies great big old faith—but what God wants us to have is sparrow faith, which is a simple, humble faith that quietly trusts God to provide for our needs. Jesus said, "Look at the sparrows." The essence of faith in God as the loving One who provides for us is not seen in the image of the person who has faith enough to move mountains, but in the image of the person who has faith as a sparrow.

Sparrows generally don't sit on a tree branch and focus the intense might of their great faith on a slab of granite in front of them so that it will move and reveal the juicy worms beneath it. No—they have sparrow faith: the simple trust and faith in God as their Source and Provider. That's it. It's not deep. It's not complicated. It's the picture of a little sparrow, a little bird that exists because it simply *must* trust its Creator to provide for its needs. Jesus is telling us that *this* is the kind of faith we need. A calm, assured faith. The faith to trust God as our complete Source and Provider for everything, at all times, without worry—

because, as it says in Philippians, "the peace of God, which transcends all understanding, will guard your hearts and your minds in Christ Jesus" (Phil. 4:7).

When I was in the Marine Corps, I often had to perform guard duty. There was a fenced perimeter they had us march around in the dark. It was late at night. Lighting was sparse. If someone approached my guard post or the area I was guarding, I had to challenge him or her by saying, "Halt! Who goes there!" Those were my general orders, to demand identification from whoever was attempting to get past me onto the base. By ordering them to identify themselves, I was establishing my authority over them, and they had to comply with my orders for identification. Once I identified myself and listened to them identify themselves, I had to determine whether or not I was going to let them past or send them on their way—I couldn't just let them loiter around. That's what guard duty was all about.

The apostle Paul says here in Philippians that the peace of God will march guard duty around your heart and mind and when the enemy comes traipsing around, the peace of God will say, "Halt! Who goes there? I represent God—who are you?" If it's peace trying to get in, then God will say, "Come on in, peace." If it's joy, He'll say, "Get in here, joy." If it's a sound mind, He'll say, "Welcome, sound mind." Mercy, happiness, love, come on in! But if it's suffering, pain or worry, the guard—the peace of God—will say, "No! You can't come around here; this is God's property. Get out!" If it's the enemy, He will say, "You can't come in here. This is God's possession. Beat it!"

The password for getting in is, "Amen and hallelujah!" The peace of God surpasses all understanding, and God provides all of our needs—worry can't come in, because God is on guard.

> Consider the lilies, how they grow: they neither toil nor spin; and yet I say to you, even Solomon in all his glory was not

> arrayed like one of these. If then God so clothes the grass, which today is in the field and tomorrow is thrown into the oven, how much more will He clothe you, O you of little faith? And do not seek what you should eat or what you should drink, nor have an anxious mind. For all these things the nations of the world seek after, and your Father knows that you need these things (Luke 12:27-30).

We don't have to manipulate God to provide for us. We don't have to try to reason or browbeat or whine or complain or cajole Him into it. You don't have to convince Him one iota to bless you—you don't deserve it anyway! God does not give because we . . .

God does not give because *we* . . .

God does not give because *we anything*! God gives because *He* is a giver. It's part of His nature to give. It's part of the essence of His character. It is an outflow of His love. He so loves that He gives. He can no more stop giving than He can stop loving.

God reveals His very nature through His names. In fact, God is even known by the name *Jehovah-Jireh*, which means, "The Lord will provide." As a provider, God doesn't merely meet several of our needs, but *all* of our needs:

> And my God shall supply *all* your need according to His riches in glory by Christ Jesus (Phil. 4:19).

The word "supply" in the verse above means *to fill up*. Where there is an emptiness, a void, a vacuum, to "supply" means to fill it. It's the same word that would be used to describe a fisherman's net being "filled up" with fish. The void of the empty net is filled with a supply of fish. When we are empty, God is the Provider who can fill us.

Blessing 3: To Multiply the Seed that Is Sown

Second Corinthians 9:10 says, "He that ministereth seed to the sower both minister bread for your food, and multiply your seed sown" (*KJV*). This indicates that the seed that you *already sowed* is also multiplied. The inference is that you have to sow the seed first before God multiplies it.

The first time Paul uses the word "seed" in this passage, it is the Greek word *sperma,* which means "something sown," such as male sperm, which leads to offspring. This means that the seed that is sown has life in it.

However, the seed that God multiplies is the *sporran* seed, which is "seed that has already been sown." He doesn't multiply the seed that we *keep,* because once you put it in the bank, you've parked it in the world's system. You have to sow it first, and then it's multiplied.

When God gives us seed, we are called to sow it. The seed that we sow always operates under the Law of the Sower. There are three parts to the Law of the Sower:

1. You only reap *what* you sow.
2. You only reap *after* you sow.
3. You always reap *more* than you sow.

God's kingdom operates through giving and receiving—as opposed to the world's system, which operates through buying and selling. In the world, you get addition from interest. But in God's kingdom, God does not simply *add* interest to what you sow, He *multiplies it.* The multiplication blessing comes from that which has already been sown.

Here's the intriguing part: God gives us seed for our need, but He doesn't stop there. He continues to pour out more and more—He takes us into *abundance*! Our blessing is a *multiplication* of that which we sowed. And since *you* determine how much you sow, *you* actually determine how much you will harvest. Thus, if you sow little, you get little.

If you sow much, you get much. If you sow nothing . . . that's right, you get nothing. (Remember the third servant!)

> God is able to make all grace abound toward you; that ye, always having all sufficiency in all things, may abound to every good work (2 Cor. 9:8, *KJV*).

In the verse above, the word "sufficiency" means "without the need of assistance." God is able to bring us to a point of sufficiency. In other words, a state in which we have no need for further assistance. It means that God becomes our full sufficiency. Because of what His grace triggers and releases into our lives, we have no further need of aid. In other words, you have within you all that you need because God's grace put it there.

Here is how the *New Revised Standard Version* puts it: "God is able to provide you with every blessing in abundance, so that by always having enough of everything, you may share abundantly in every good work." Simple. To the point. Clear. Powerful.

God says that it is His will that every need we ever have will be met in Him so that beyond Him we have no need. Not everyone accepts that grace. Not all people choose to abide in God's grace. But God says that your relationship with Him is so important to Him that it is His heart's desire to meet every need you'll ever face. Sufficiency speaks of a psychological contentment and emotional satisfaction, because you know that you will never face a need that cannot be met by your Father. It speaks about peace. When God says "all sufficiency," it means you're settled. You're satisfied. You're content. Then you can focus on giving to others—those in need.

Blessing 4: To Increase the Fruits of Our Righteousness

God doesn't stop at mere sufficiency—He gives in *abundance*! Second Corinthians 9:8 says that we may "abound to every good work." We can be confident when placing our trust in Him, because He is a God of abundance, completely unaffected by finite supplies.

The kingdom of God operates on giving and receiving, whereas the world's system operates on buying and selling. The world's system, which is controlled by the spirit of mammon (money), operates on the principle that there is a finite supply—a scarcity—of goods, and that those goods must therefore be tightly controlled only by a certain few: the haves, who are bent on the dual goal of gaining more to hoard and keeping it out of the hands of the have-nots. The principle behind the operation of the world system is that *there's only so much*, but the principle behind the operation of God's kingdom is that *there's an abundance.* This principle is revealed in the progression of the entire 2 Corinthians 9:8-12 text as a movement from one degree up to the next.

God's goal is not mere sufficiency, but abundance. God wants to go beyond simply meeting your needs and into blessing you abundantly. He transfers us from one level of provision (which is represented in our relationship with Him) to the next. As we get a grip on one level—as we grow closer to Him in trust, love and obedience—we then move up to the next level. God's goal is not to make us merely sufficient, but to release favor and grace in order that we "may abound." In other words, that we might have *plenty*.

Here is how the different translations state 2 Corinthians 9:8 (emphasis added):

- God is willing to release favor upon you so that you will have *all that you need* (*NIV*).

- That you might have *an abundance* (*NKJV*).

- That you'll *always have everything you need and plenty left over to share with others* (*NLT*).

- That you will possess *enough to require no aid or support and furnished in abundance for every good work and charitable donation* (*AMP*).

- That you will have *everything you need and more so that there will not only be enough for your own needs but plenty left over to give joyfully to others* (*TLB*).

The revelation is that *God desires to be your Source*. Any time we look to or expect anything or anybody else to supply any of our needs, we've desecrated our relationship with God, who says, "I am the need-meeter here—I'm the One who does the blessing."

> Where is the man who fears the Lord? God will teach him to choose the best. He shall live within God's circle of blessing (Ps. 25:12–13, *TLB*).

If God follows the text that He has revealed in 2 Corinthians 9, then He will take you beyond sufficiency and into abundance, blessing you past your need. Then, when your sown seeds are multiplied, you will begin living within "God's circle of blessing"—and *that* is where God desires that we live. Within that circle, every need and every obligation we have is fully provided for.

Picture the circle as the top of a cup. There comes a point in the cup at which all the needs are met, the cup is full—but *He keeps on pouring*! And as He pours, we get drenched by the overflow.

According to Scripture, these blessings are varied in scope and content. In addition to monetary blessings, they include:

- *Wisdom and knowledge:* "Oh, the depth of the riches both of the wisdom and knowledge of God!" (Rom. 11:33).

- *Understanding:* "The eyes of your understanding being enlightened; that you may know what is the hope of His calling, what are the riches of the glory of His inheritance in the saints" (Eph. 1:18).

- *Grace and kindness:* "That in the ages to come He might show the exceeding riches of His grace in His kindness toward us in Christ Jesus" (Eph. 2:7).

- *Encouragement*: "That their hearts may be encouraged, being knit together in love, and attaining to all riches of the full assurance of understanding, to the knowledge of the mystery of God, both of the Father and of Christ" (Col. 2:2).

When we are living in God's circle of blessing, all of these blessings become ours. His wisdom and knowledge, His understanding, His grace and kindness, His encouragement and even the knowledge of the mystery of God. In other words, *all* of our needs are met by Him. He provides for us abundantly, above and beyond our basic needs, so that we are truly living in the overflow of His blessings. Abundance means over and above, more than enough, beyond our needs.

I'm going to go for the overflow myself. I want to live in the abundance. I don't want my family to live scrimping and scraping from day to day. I don't want to be begging and pleading. I want to get into a position where God moves me from sufficiency to overflow! And not only for myself, but because when I'm in the overflow, I'm in Kingdom territory and He can use me as a channel to turn around and bless others in His kingdom!

Blessing 5: To Give

In 2 Corinthians 9:6-7, Paul writes, "But this I say, He which soweth sparingly shall reap also sparingly; and he which soweth bountifully shall reap also bountifully. Every man according as he purposeth in his heart, so let him give; not grudgingly, or of necessity: for God loveth a cheerful giver" (*KJV*).

Money counts when it is used as a resource to be released, rather than as a commodity to be gathered. One of the greatest financial decisions you will make in your lifetime is how you will handle the overflow from God. Unfortunately, most people consume the abundance on themselves. Mammon steps in and so influences some people that it transforms their *need* into *greed*. But God is clear on how we are to handle the overflow: We are to take these blessings and give toward the needs of others—and cheerfully!

Everybody has needs: need for food, need for shelter, need for clothing and so on. There are obligations that we each have, as well. For example, my sister, my brother and I have an obligation to our mother (who, at this writing, is 91 years old). We're not trusting anybody to do that job—not the president in the White House, not the governor, not the mayor. We depend on each other to take care of our mother. That obligation has become a need to us, a need to minister to and serve our mother. If God does not bless us at a certain level, we will not be able to fulfill that obligation. Sufficiency is what enables us to meet our personal needs and obligations, which include providing for our mother. I can't trust any congressman to take care of my momma. No U.S. senator went through any pain to bring me into the world. *I'm* going to take care of my momma. That's my job, my obligation. And that's where God's overflow comes in.

God says that it is the *Kingdom* that is to be blessed by your overflow. That is, the needs of others in the Kingdom, those whose cup is not as full as yours, whose harvest was not as abundant as yours. Overflow is when God says, "I bless you. Now I want to use you to bless somebody else." God did not bless you just to give you a new car and a bigger house and a bigger bank account. He blessed you to meet your needs, to start accomplishing some of your heart's desires, to give to the expanding of various ministries and *to bless people who have needs*.

Sadly, most people never reach the overflow, or once they do, they consume the overflow on themselves. The contemporary theology of prosperity has so poisoned the spirit of much of the Church today that we have become narcissistic, selfish and stingy when it comes to anything outside ourselves. We have come to believe that the only reason God blesses me is for *me*. This extremist theology of prosperity has infected the Church with selfishness, blindness and tunnel vision, ultimately distorting our very relationship with God Himself, because we've begun looking to Him as only existing to give us *stuff*. What appears to be a spiritual relationship with God is simply spiritual manipulation, our trying to get more stuff from Him.

That's why God's measurement is not about the size of the check in your account or the amount of currency in your offering envelope. It's about the size of your *heart*. If you have a heart for the Kingdom, you cannot help but have a desire and a concern for people outside of yourself.

Kingdom Business on Earth

In the natural world, treasure brings forth treasure. In the spirit realm, the same principle holds true. The Kingdom expands through Kingdom business. "Doing Kingdom business" consists of the procreation of, the multiplication of, the spreading of, God's Word.

When you make the decision to invest, *to do business*, and you are prepared to take advantage of business opportunities as they arise, they *will* arise! Here is just one personal example.

God has called our church to do something that cannot be done merely through tithes and offerings. It's much bigger than that. Some of our offerings are used to invest and turn a profit. For example, our church building was placed into a for-profit corporation owned by the church. The building, which is a very large professional sports arena, is used during non-church hours to generate profits, via rental for business and public use such as concerts, family entertainment and corporate events. Those profits are then fed back into the Kingdom enterprise, which for us consists of various activities that Faithful Central Bible Church conducts to expand God's kingdom while simultaneously serving the needs of His children.

Faithful Central Bible Church is a willing instrument in God's hands in expanding the influence of His kingdom on Earth. Our doing business by following God's process for making His money grow has created jobs in our community, put food on tables and given incomes to workers. It has given single mothers money for baby milk and diapers and food and shelter. It has helped provide homes for families. All these needs are being met because of a building not owned by a secular landlord nor by a faceless corporate entity, but by the Children of Light, by the very chosen of God, by people who are bold enough to realize how big our God is and to act accordingly.

Likewise, your money—on any level, big or small—is to be used to advance God's plans and purposes, to bless His children and to be a light of example to nonbelievers.

Profit is never to be hoarded. It is to be used to expand God's kingdom, to further His glory and to spread His glorious gospel message. *That* is why we are called to do Kingdom business here on Earth.

All across the nation, everywhere I go, people cannot believe that a church is being used to turn a profit in the secular world. But why should they be so surprised? Doing business and making a profit is a biblical concept. After all, does not the Word of God say, "The wealth of the sinner is stored up for the righteous" (Prov. 13:22)?

God's heart is to bless you. If you will allow Him to do so, if you will seek His heart and follow His ways, He has a great abundance stored up for you!

Chapter 5

The Purpose of Money

Money is the central medium God uses to supply our material needs. There are several different purposes for money apart from the obvious use as a common medium of barter or exchange within a culture.

Some of the Purposes of Money

The *purposes* of money are different than (but related to) the *blessings* of money, which we examined in the previous chapter. Let's take a look at some of these purposes.

To Motivate Christian Unity

God uses money as a way to motivate Christian unity. As we use money to bless others, we are joined together in a common goal, which encourages and promotes unity within the Body of Christ. As a result of unity, those who have much will share with those who have little.

I believe the welfare system in America exists because the Church is no longer doing the job of caring for God's flock. Apart from a few charity organizations and mission efforts that don't take an exorbitant percentage for operating overhead, Christians rarely take care of people who are indigent or hurting. They rarely provide for those who are struggling or suffering. They rarely seek out those in need. They're too busy focusing on themselves, their wants, their needs, their personal "five year plan."

One of the biggest uses of state and federal income taxes is to provide for the needs of people on welfare. If we Christians were doing our job better, perhaps our government would not be forced to step in. The welfare system has now become the norm—but it didn't used to be this way (see Acts 2:45; 4:35).

The enemy has managed to change attitudes and values to the point that we are a culture with an *everyone for himself* mentality and a *stash and hoard* approach to money. This should not be. The Church must be unified and take care of each other, and use money to bless and aid those around us.

To Manifest God's Power

We are told in Deuteronomy, "Remember the LORD your God, for it is He who gives you power to get wealth, that He may establish His covenant which He swore to your fathers, as it is this day" (8:18). This verse stands as a reminder that whatever we have, we have only because God gave us the power to get it. Whatever you make in the form of income, you make because God gave you the ability to do so.

The Church of Laodicea denied their need for God (see Rev. 3:15-18). They were poor and wretched and in need, but they claimed they were fine, insisting that they didn't need God. It's similar to when your child reaches those teen years and starts thinking she doesn't need any parents. She goes off on her own and finds out pretty quickly that life is much tougher fending for herself than she imagined.

Our needs become opportunities for God to prove Himself to us. When we have needs but we deny Him the opportunity to provide for us, to be there for us, to prove His Word to us, then we are denying His very existence.

To Manifest God's Goodness

Proverbs reminds us to "trust in the LORD with all your heart, and lean not on your own understanding; in all your ways acknowledge Him, and He shall direct your paths" (3:5-6). When we trust the

Lord and acknowledge that He is our God, He directs, leads and guides us. He doesn't *have* to—He's not *obligated* to do this. But in His goodness, because He is a good God, He promises to direct our paths. And the truth is, as difficult as we can be, God loves providing for us, caring for us, loving us and offering us hope—and a process for financial security!

To Maintain Faithfulness

God uses money as a blessing to maintain our faithfulness. He promises to meet our needs and He gives us the means to do so. He says, "Here's the provision, here's your needs being met. I've done what I said I would do. I performed My work." In this way, money is a means by which God demonstrates *His own* faithfulness to us—He uses it to show what a faithful God He is. Once He has done His part, He watches to see if we'll remain faithful to Him.

According to Proverbs 3:6, it's only when we acknowledge Him that He will direct our paths. Inherent in that *quid pro quo* is a challenge to us to be faithful to Him in all aspects of our lives—including finances.

To Mature the Saints

As we learn His process and trust God to meet our financial needs, we grow in wisdom and in spiritual maturity. This maturing process is progressive: As God meets our needs, we learn to trust Him more; and as we discover that we can trust Him more, we tend to step out in even more faith and obey Him even more.

Being able to look back over your life and see God's pattern of providence for you is a "track record" that gives you increasing security that God always has (and thus always will) provide for you—particularly as you press in to Him in obedience. This process of provision leads to a maturing in your life and an increasing ability to trust that He's got your back and will *always* do what He says.

Here is what I call the "When-Then" Spiritual Maturity Flowchart:

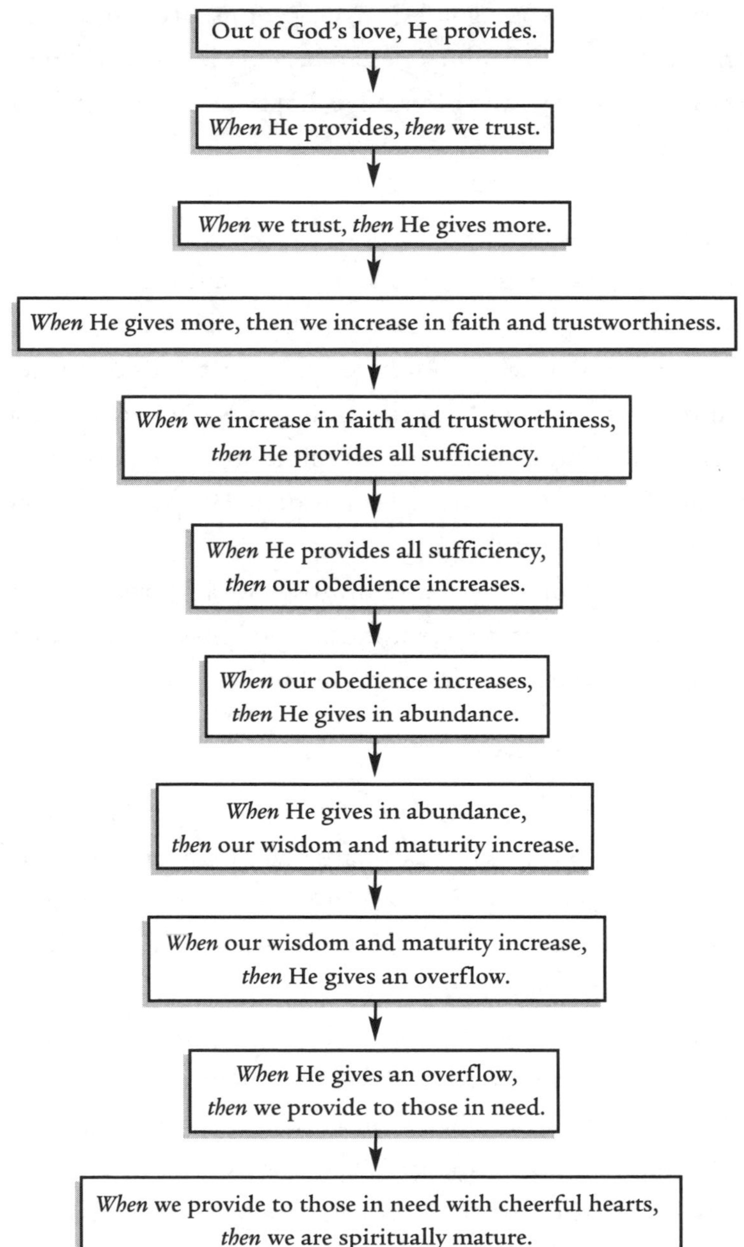

As this flowchart indicates, money counts when it flows *through us*, beyond simply coming to us or stopping with us.

To Minster to the World

Ministry and outreaches cost money. That's just the way things work in this world. If we're going to lead people to the Lord, we need the funding to do so. God gives us the ability to gain money in order to minister to the world.

Who Meets Your Needs?

Paul tells us that God is able to make "all grace abound" toward us and that He gives us sufficiency in all things. This is a theme repeated throughout Scripture. We are promised over and over that our Father will direct our paths and provide for our needs. He knows what our needs are even before we ask Him—even before *we* know what our needs are!—and He's able and willing to supply our needs. But first, He desires relationship, fellowship, with us. After all, He's not some wishing-well—He's the *Person* who meets our needs!

According to Proverbs 3:6, it is after we've trusted in the Lord with our whole hearts and acknowledged Him that He directs our paths and provides for us. He provides for our needs as our behavior glorifies Him. However, He even provides for us by giving us His wisdom (via the Bible) before we follow Him—if only we will pick the Bible up and study it. Sadly, most Christians don't study the Word on their own, and many that do relegate their Bible reading to whatever the preacher says for 35 to 45 minutes (or less) from the pulpit on Sunday morning—*if* they attend regularly.[1]

The question is, which needs do you take to God? Most people take only those needs they can't handle themselves. The ones we think we can handle, we try to handle on our own, cutting God out of the relationship as our need-meeter. How many times have you thought you could take care of something yourself, only to find yourself making the situation worse? We've all been there. The solution is to *come to God first.* Always include Him in on matters, regardless of whether or not you think you can handle it yourself. That's what relationship is all about.

Obedient Receiving

Your need becomes the seed for your miracle. We miss God's blessings when we either refuse His provision or when we try to supply our own needs. Doing that means that we aren't trusting God enough; we aren't walking in an all-inclusive faith. As a prominent pastor once said, "You don't trust God until you have to." Our tendency is to turn to God only when we've gotten ourselves into a mess. When we "use" God that way, our need becomes our only point of contact with Him. When we deny His meeting our needs on an ongoing basis, we miss out on experiencing regular, ongoing blessings from Him and we severely limit our relationship with Him.

There's no sin in having a need. The issue with God is in how we have them met. Are your methods of having your needs met pleasing to Him? Some people choose ways that dishonor God. For example, a dating couple may decide that they're having an overabundance of financial difficulty, so they move in with each other—they "shack up"—using the excuse that they'll be able to pool resources, save a little money together and in a few months get out of debt. The final goal (getting out of debt) is good—the means to do so is not. That's not God's way of being an "obedient receiver" of His providence.

Let's take a look at the five components of being an obedient receiver from God. These include: (1) allowing God to define your need; (2) allowing God to determine your provision; (3) allowing God to determine the timing of your provision; (4) receiving the supply before you use it; and (5) handling the supply God's way.

1. Allow God to Define Your Need

One of the devil's tricks is to get us to meet our own needs—he loves cutting us away from any potential relationship activity with God. People often define as needs things that aren't truly needs. Many times what we *think* we need is exactly what we *don't* need (and can actually be to our detriment). This is a sly trick of the enemy, who comes along and disguises our *wants* to look like our *needs*. It is God who *defines* the need. It is Satan who *disguises* the need.

God knows what we need and what we don't. For example, it is a need for families to spend quality time together, more than Dad working a second job in order to pay for more possessions. If there is a need, God will supply it. Conversely, if He doesn't supply it, then maybe it wasn't a need. If you've prayed about a particular issue and His answer is no, then maybe it wasn't a need, but just a greed.

For instance, when Faithful Central Bible Church purchased the Great Western Forum, we knew we were going to have to trust God to provide for it. But we also knew it was a need—we were expanding and growing, and needed much more space. We put it in God's hands and He provided for it. If He hadn't provided the financing, then that would have indicated that the building wasn't a need according to God's definition of need. Why? Because God always provides for a true need—it may not be our image of how the need should be provided for, but He *always* provides.

2. Allow God to Determine Your Provision

Let God meet your need *His* way. We don't dictate to Him; *He* determines how our need is best met. For example, if you need a car, let God provide you with a car. If He provides it, you *know* you will be able to pay for it. Don't try to keep up with the next-door neighbor and get a loan that you can't afford for a brand-new Mercedes when you can do fine with a previously owned Toyota. It may be better to start with the

Toyota and move up than to start with what you can't afford and watch the re-po man downsize you!

Allow God to determine what the provision will be, and be grateful for the provision, no matter what it is. If God provides you with that new Mercedes Benz or Lexus, then fine—those are solid, reliable automobiles—but let Him be the one who clearly provides it for you. A rule of thumb for recognizing whether or not it's God who is doing the providing is *ease*: God won't make it an unbearable or even destructive struggle for you to obtain something like an automobile. Too many of us spend money we don't have to buy things we don't need to impress people we don't even know!

3. Allow God to Determine the Timing of Your Provision

God best knows when the need must be met.

When God first made His covenant with Abraham, Abraham thought He was too old to ever have children (see Gen. 15:1-3). Finally, when Abraham was in his 80s and nothing had happened yet, he decided to take matters into his own hands and he had a child named Ishmael with Hagar, Sarah's servant (see Gen. 16). Because Abraham took matters into his own hands, the Middle East has been in turmoil for centuries—all because Abraham didn't wait on God.

If God says He's going to do it, how long are you willing to wait for Him to carry out His word? *Learn to wait on the Lord!* Only impatient, undisciplined children refuse to wait. God *will* do what He says, in His perfect timing.

4. Receive the Supply Before You Use It

We must receive God's provision before we use it. It's like window-shopping: If you know you don't have the money, why go window shopping? By the time you get home, you'll have an armful of stuff, and the only way you got it was with credit or by spending money earmarked for something necessary.

When you use the supply before you receive it, you're saying, "That's okay. I have faith. I have faith that God will supply the money before the bill is due." You may have faith—and faith is certainly good—but a misapplied faith leads to misbehaving with your money. We have many in our ministry who have learned the pain of foreclosure, repossession and bankruptcy by spending money before they received it—money they really didn't have.

5. Handle the Supply God's Way

When God supplies the need, you have an obligation to handle the provision in a way that is pleasing to Him. Many people are not having their needs met because they spend on their *wants* the money that God meant for their *needs*. It all belongs to Him in the first place, so handle it *His* way.

The purpose of money is not without reason. Once we begin to recognize God's intentions surrounding money, once we start to see how He works behind, within and around the concept of money and its use, and once we grasp His wisdom surrounding the proper use of money, a glimpse of God's desire for His children emerges:

> You shall expand to the right and to the left, and your descendants will inherit the nations (Isa. 54:3).

Note

1. This totals 3 hours per month. There are approximately 487 *waking* hours in each month, which means that most people spend less than 1 percent of their entire waking time getting to know God through the study of His Word.

Chapter 6

What About the Tithe?

"Bring all the tithes into the storehouse,
that there may be food in My house, and try Me now in this," says the Lord *of hosts,*
"If I will not open for you the windows of Heaven and pour out for you such blessing
that there will not be room enough to receive it."

Malachi 3:10

Before we move on to the next section, let's deal with the tithe.

The principle of the tithe is a principle of *priority*. It is a tangible declaration that God is first in your life. It says that you acknowledge God as the source of your resources and you put Him first in your stewardship of what He brings into your life. In a very simple way, stewardship is how you handle what God gives you to manage or control. A steward manages property that belongs to another. God owns it all. We affirm His ownership by giving to Him up front, off the top of our income—which He brings into our lives.

The word "tithe" speaks of the first-fruits, or the first crops harvested, that were to be deposited into a storehouse. The storehouse around the time of the prophet Malachi, some 2,455 years ago, had a similar function to that of our modern-day grain silos. The metaphor in Malachi 3:10 is that of an agrarian society—when the harvest came in, the best part of the crop went into the storehouse.

The original Hebrew word for "tithe" in this passage is *ma'aser*, meaning "a tenth part" or "payment of a tenth part." In other words, according to Malachi 3:10, the tenth part of our increase, our earnings, are deposited in the storehouse of God.

As indicated in the passage below, during the seven years of plenty before the famine, when Joseph had power over all the land of Egypt, he stored up the wealth of the land by putting it into great storehouses:

> Now in the seven plentiful years the ground brought forth abundantly. So he gathered up all the food of the seven years which were in the land of Egypt, and laid up the food in the cities; he laid up in every city the food of the fields which surrounded them. Joseph gathered very much grain, as the sand of the sea, until he stopped counting, for it was immeasurable (Gen. 41:47-49).

Christians bicker and banter about the tithe because churches today are teaching an incomplete gospel on this topic, too. "Tithing is old school," people claim. "We don't still have to pay that, do we?" Or they clutch their wallet and wonder, "That's not in the New Testament, is it?"

The Tithe: A Brief History

The background of tithing is fascinating. Once you understand its purpose, its history and its modern relevance to our salvation, you gain a fresh new point of view on this amazing tool of God.

> After Abram returned from defeating Kedorlaomer and the kings allied with him, the king of Sodom came out to meet him in the Valley of Shaveh (that is, the King's Valley). Then Melchizedek king of Salem brought out bread and wine. He was priest of God Most High, and he blessed Abram, saying, "Blessed

> be Abram by God Most High, Creator of heaven and earth. And blessed be God Most High, who delivered your enemies into your hand." Then Abram gave him a tenth of everything (Gen.14:17-20, *NIV*).

In Genesis 14, when Abram (before God changed his name to Abraham) was living in Hebron near the great trees of Mamre, his nephew Lot was taken prisoner by several Persian kings who had journeyed to Sodom to put down a rebellion.

Abram set out with 318 of his servants, who were also trained as soldiers (which says much about the tumultuous times of the region) to rescue Lot. They pursued the Persians, caught up with them and freed Lot.

As he was returning victorious, Abram encountered the king of Salem, a priest named Melchizedek (whose name means "my king is righteous"), who worshiped Jehovah. Melchizedek honored Abram with a banquet of wine and bread, and Abram responded to the generosity and blessing of Melchizedek by honoring him with a tithe on the spoils he had captured from the Persian kings during his rescue of Lot. Thus, tithing began as a response to a blessing from Melchizedek, a king and priest of God, to Abram, a wealthy and powerful man.

In Genesis 12, God told Abraham, "I will bless you"—and in Genesis 14, God does so. In chapter 12, God made the promise; in chapter 14, He fulfilled the promise.

Although the actual tithe began with Abraham and the priest Melchizedek, the *structure* of the tithe began with Moses. Moses affirmed the tithe and the structures for it—the different forms of the tithe, the grain offerings, sheep and livestock offerings, and so on—were all put into place.

As history indicates, the tithe didn't begin with a law; it began with Abram's gratitude to God as the Source of his victory, and Abram's honoring the blessing given him by the king-priest Melchizedek by giving Melchizedek (as a representative of God) a portion of the spoils.

Thus, the establishment of the tithe involved:

- *A person*: Abram
- *A principle*: God will provide
- *A priest*: The priest-king Melchizedek (an archetype of Jesus)
- *A promise*: The nation Israel shall come from Abraham's loins and that they shall be blessed

In Genesis 17, God makes the actual covenant with Abram to make him the father of many nations, changing his name from Abram (which means "father of loftiness or stature") to Abraham (meaning "father of a multitude"). God tells him, "I will establish My covenant between Me and you and your descendants after you in their generations, for an everlasting covenant, to be God to you and your descendants after you" (Gen. 17:7).

This meant that the covenant blessing was with Abraham's seed as well, making it valid far beyond Abraham to all of his descendants, as a will and testament from God. Abraham's seed, his line of descendants, the nation of Israel, received the covenant promise. The promise was that all of his descendants would be blessed.[1]

Love Gone Cold

However, what began to happen with the people of Israel was that their love for God started to wane. Instead of giving their tithe as the best, the first-fruits, off the top, the cream of the crop, they started giving less than the best. Their love was growing cold and they began to give the lame cows to sacrifice, the sheep with a bad leg, the doves with a broken wing, instead of giving God their best.

God noticed that their love was growing cold. Yet even though they had turned away from Him and were giving less than honorable sacrifices, they kept coming to Him, though they were only going through the motions. They were still bringing their tithe, but now it was the old, one-eyed, broken-down offerings they were giving to the Lord—like a married person who has someone on the side but who still wants to keep his or her spouse in the picture just for appearance's sake.

Same Game, Different Players

Hundreds of years later, in the book of Hebrews, we learn that, with the coming of Messiah, things changed. Jesus is now our high priest, after the order of Melchizedek:

> And having been perfected, He became the author of eternal salvation to all who obey Him, called by God as High Priest "according to the order of Melchizedek," of whom we have much to say, and hard to explain, since you have become dull of hearing (Heb. 5:9-11).

In the passage above, Jesus is identified as a priest forever, in the order of Melchizedek, thus making Christ the Person, the Principle, the Priest and the Promise—all embodied in One—whereas, back in Genesis, the person was Abram, the principle was that God will provide, the priest was Melchizedek and the promise was that the nation Israel would come from Abraham's loins and would be blessed. Because Jesus hadn't yet come when the covenant was first established, Melchizedek was a "stand in," so to speak, until the time came for Jesus to appear on the scene in Bethlehem. Abram brought the tithe to the High Priest Melchizedek, thus plugging Abram into the covenant promise of God's generational blessing of descendants forever.

The tithe became the connection with the covenant. The tithe was the *switch* that activated it all, putting things into gear.

With the book of Hebrews, and now with us in this generation, only the players have changed: Instead of the person being Abraham, the person is Abraham's seed (us). Instead of Melchizedek being the priest, Jesus is the priest. Instead of Melchizedek receiving the tithe, if Jesus is your Lord, He receives the tithe.

When you bring the tithe, you are plugged into the promise of the blessing as well. The tithe is still the principle (the "rules of the game," so to speak) and is still brought to the "priest" (the Church). The game is the same. The players are different.

Tithe and Offering: The Difference

There's a difference between the tithe and the offering. The tithe is the portion that goes to direct ministry-related efforts. In our culture today, the tithe would be the amount or percentage that you give to the church where you are being spiritually fed. This money supports the operational structure of that church.

The offering, on the other hand, is an amount of money that you give over and above the tithe. This is money that you donate for specific causes your church is involved in or ministries or charities that are separate from your church. You determine the amount of your offerings and you determine which ministries you want to give to, but offerings are always *in addition to* the tithe:

> Every devoted offering is most holy to the LORD . . . And all the tithe of the land, whether of the seed of the land or of the fruit of the tree, is the LORD's. It is holy to the LORD (Lev. 27:28,30).

The word "devoted" in Leviticus 27:28 is the Hebrew word *cherem*. It means "consecrated," something that is dedicated to someone and only that person can say how it is to be used.

There are two things we must understand about the tithe: First, the tenth part brings with it a fiduciary responsibility (that is, a responsibility to manage what God owns and has entrusted to us) that we must handle it in a way that honors God. Second, the tithe is holy unto the Lord. God declares the tithe and offering as holy unto Him. They are devoted, set aside, consecrated. He alone determines how they are to be used.

Handling your "seed" in a way that causes it to accrue in your spiritual account with God is acknowledging that it belongs to God. We don't give God the tithe—we *return it back to Him*. Therefore, it is holy. As such, God watches how we handle what He has entrusted into our care.

If you always give your tithes first, your offering will be honored by God. If you are not tithing, then when you give offerings, they may be accepted but they cannot be *honored* by God. In other words, they carry no residual blessings effects toward you in the future.

When we withhold a tithe, we are actually stealing from God, as the Scripture below plainly tells us: "Will a man rob God? Yet you have robbed Me! But you say, 'In what way have we robbed You?' In tithes and offerings" (Mal. 3:8).

What would happen if there was a God patrol that came around flashing badges and arresting people for everything they have that is stolen property? If you have things that you bought for yourself (that you probably didn't even need!) and you haven't been paying your tithes, then that means you have been buying things with money that you withheld from God, money that doesn't belong to you. In a sense, it is stolen property. God takes note of things like that. He calls it "robbery." In every state in America, robbery is a felony, punishable by incarceration in prison!

This stealing from is what Malachi is referring to when he quoted God's saying, "You have robbed me in tithes and offerings!" You have taken God's percentage and put it into your own pocket while calling yourself one of His. You're not doing as God says in His Word. You're keeping His money for yourself.

It is interesting that God calls this robbery. He doesn't call it burglary. One significant difference between burglary and robbery is that burglaries usually occur when something is stolen and the thief is not seen. Homes are normally burglarized while the owners are away. However, God says that when we refuse to bring the tithe, we *rob* Him. Robberies occur when the thief steals something from a person and the thief is seen. Often you are robbed while you are looking at the person—even looking him straight in the eye. God seems to say that when you refuse to bring the tithe, you are not burglarizing Him (as if He couldn't see it), instead you are robbing Him—looking Him straight in His eyes—often while asking Him to bless you more! *Would a man rob God?*

Everything we have was given to us by God. It's *His*. Tithing is about our hearts, our attitudes, as shown by a gesture of giving back to Him in acknowledgment that we're in continual, right relationship with Him. When we start hanging on to what's His and giving nothing in return, what is He to do? How is He to treat us then? What do you do with the teenage child who lives at home and doesn't help, doesn't do any chores, doesn't have a part-time job, doesn't sweep up, doesn't clean, doesn't contribute a thing, and yet wants your help—or worse, is taking cash out of your wallet or purse! As the "sovereign" in the family, as the parent, what do you do?

Tithing began as an affirmation of the sovereignty of God, in celebration of a victory given by God to Abraham. The tithe was initiated from an attitude of gratitude for the victories the Lord had granted His children. In this same way, we tithe today in affirmation of the sovereignty of God in our everyday lives. It is our declaration that He is our provider and protector.

With Jesus, we had a switch of players, but the rules of the game are still the same. We are still to bring the tithe, but now we bring it to Jesus, our High Priest forever. Instead of Abraham bringing the tithe, it's now the Church that brings it. Same game, different players.

Where Now?

In today's culture, the tithe is to go to the place where God channels our spiritual provision, where we are planted and growing in the Word, where we are spiritually fed, such as our home church.

Some Christians eat all over town. They go first to this church, then to that one, then to another one down the road. Regardless of this grazing, the tithe is to be planted where we receive our spiritual nurturing. Where we are growing in faith. Where we are being taught in the Word. Where we are serving and being together with other Christians in community. Where we are being held accountable by fellow Christians, being empowered by the Spirit of God and being changed by His Word.

If we followed the biblical pattern of tithing to the letter, we would actually give over 20 percent of our income. There were two tithes paid annually and one paid every three years. As indicated earlier, the word "tithe" means "a tenth" or "a tenth part." Technically, you can't tithe more than 10 percent. You can give more than one tithe (as the Israelites did), but you can't really tithe 12 percent or 18 percent, because the word means "a tenth." Everything above the tenth is considered an "offering." The least amount indicated is the tithe. (However, an example of the least amount of offering given is found in Mark 12:42, where the widow gave two mites–*THE MESSAGE* translation says, "a measly two cents." But that two mites was 100 percent of what the widow had! She gave more than the tithe of 10 percent; she gave her all.)

Today, how much you should give above the tithe is between you and God. He could have said 30 percent. He could have said 5. But it's not about *amount;* it's about *attitude.* It's about turning the heart around and giving back to God whatever He requests, to show that He is first and foremost in our lives. It's a token action that physically demonstrates what's in our hearts: the knowledge that He owns it all and that He deserves the first and the best.

It's not so much about the percentage; the main thing is your attitude. If "honoring" to you means 20 percent or 40 percent or 60 percent or 90 percent, then that's what you give. Never let people manipulate you into giving, because God won't honor that motivation. It must be from *your* heart.

Good Soil Versus Bad

"Sowing" is an agrarian or farm term referring to planting. God has created a system that is self-sustaining, always growing and moving forward. When we bring our tithe into the storehouse today, we're *sowing*. We take the first-fruits that we've harvested (which is our tithe, or the *seed*) and we sow it into the storehouse (which is the *soil*, or where we tithe to) so that it can multiply and grow even more.

The key to successful sowing is not in the seed alone. It is also related to the type of "soil" the seed is planted into. Even the best seed fails to bring forth a crop if it is deposited into bad soil. In other words, be diligent about putting your tithe into the soil of good, solid ministries whose backgrounds, key personnel and leadership you have researched, as well as the percentage of giving that goes to meet needs after the overhead expenses of the organization. It makes no sense to give to a charity or ministry that keeps an exorbitant portion of the donations for its operational costs and overhead, with little going to the objects of the ministry's focus.

Tithing Specifics

While the tithe isn't a quick fix for financial problems, it *is* something we're called to do. The tithe is to be given right when we get it, because we are to honor God with our first-fruits. Although it is certainly not the alpha and omega of our relationship with our Lord, it is a great and tangible indicator of where the Lord falls in our list of priorities. God wants to be first. Tithing is one way we can show that He is.

Not only does God deserve our first-fruits, but He also commands us to have no other gods before Him (see Exod. 20:3, *KJV*). When we give God our first-fruits, we are declaring and affirming that He is first, He is our God and there is no other before Him in our lives.

Apart from its historical context, the tithe has three central contemporary applications: (1) to provide for the ministry; (2) to keep the enemy at bay; and (3) to promote faith. Let's examine each of these.

1. The Tithe Provides for the Ministry

Deuteronomy and Nehemiah talk about the fact that the tithe, which included food and all the other items that were brought to the temple, provided for the priests, the gatekeepers, the musicians, the Levites, strangers in need, orphans and widows. In the same way, today's tithe promotes ministry; provides food, resources and support for priests; and takes care of people in need.

Nowhere in Scripture is the tithe said to be used for a building fund. The tabernacle and the temple were not built by tithe monies—the funds to build the temple and tabernacle came from offerings over and above the tithe.

2. The Tithe Keeps the Enemy at Bay

When we retain riches that are earmarked for the Kingdom, those riches become a target for the enemy. Worse than that, once we have more than we need, *we* become a target for the enemy!

The devil never lets up on us. If your excess beyond your need is not earmarked, set aside, designated, for building more wealth for God's kingdom or for building an inheritance for your children's children, then paint a big red bull's-eye on that money, because it is a juicy target for the enemy.

However, if you identify early on that 10 percent *always* goes to God, another certain percentage *always* goes to creating wealth and another percentage *always* goes to offerings, then the enemy can't trip you up no matter how he tries. Once you've earmarked those funds and have made up your mind about where they're going, the enemy can only try to tempt you in that area—but his efforts to sidetrack you become feeble and ineffective and you can chuckle and shrug him off. God says he will protect your harvest from the enemy (see Mal. 3:11).

3. The Tithe Promotes Faith

Many people treat the tithe like a burden. This is due to a lack of understanding that it is actually the doorway to great blessing, because the tithe promotes faith, and faith does not go unrewarded! It is one of the ways we demonstrate the preeminence of God in our lives.

Many people don't tithe because they fear that if they give God one-tenth of the money He gave them, then they'll run short somewhere else. He's only asking for a measly 10 percent, yet they're afraid they can't make it on 90 percent? That's obviously a spirit of fear controlled by a spirit of mammon. The irrational fear of not making ends meet on 90 percent of God's provision comes only from the devil. Reject it! It's the enemy and the enemy alone who tries to convince you that if you tithe you can't make it on 90 percent. But God says that you can't make it on 90 percent if you *don't* tithe! Who are you going to believe?

Then there are the people who fear *not* tithing back to God what is due to Him because they're afraid they might miss what they think is due to them! This is a fear based on law and works.

These fears and misplaced motivations should be neither the drive nor the impediment to tithe. Tithe because you love God. Tithe because you wouldn't rob someone you love. Tithe because God asks us to. Plain and simple.

Tithing reminds us that God is first. When we tithe and give Him the first of our income, it is a constant reminder that it's for Him, because He is first, number one in our lives above all. We are humbling ourselves, telling Him, "You brought me to this place; You gave me all that I have—my home, my family, my income, the ability to get wealth."

It is God's love that prompts us to give, because He is the great Giver. It is our faith that responds to His love, because we trust His Word. God so loves that He releases favor. God so loves that He releases grace. When I see demonstrations of the perfect love and provision of God and when I do what He calls me to do, I am able to stand in the face of the devil and the spirit of mammon and declare, "You are a liar!" Have faith that God will do everything He says He will do.

The only way to cast out fear concerning your provision is simply to trust God. Trust promotes faith and protects us from the influence of mammon. Trust allows us to see God doing what our calculator says cannot be done. Countless Christians trust God with their giving and are doing *more* with the 90 percent that's left than they did with the entire 100 percent!

From Genesis through Revelation, tithing proves yet another foundation for our faith in God. In all that Scripture, there's only one place where God *challenges* us to trust Him—one place! Malachi 3:10 says, "Bring ye all the tithes into the storehouse, that there may be meat in mine house, and prove me now herewith, saith the LORD of hosts, if I will not open you the windows of Heaven, and pour you out a blessing, that there shall not be room enough to receive it" (*KJV*).

What the Tithe Is Not

Sometimes tithing is taught with the idea that once you tithe everything is going to be fine. It doesn't work that way. Contrary to these teachings, the tithe is not a quick fix to financial problems. Tithing does not remove the curse of debt from your life. That only happens once we repent and start behaving responsibly with our money, our business and our finances.

If you are tithing off of your income but still spending more than you earn, tithing won't help. If you start tithing today but don't pay your bills, you will still get bad credit, you will still have money problems and you will have neutralized the potential positive effects of tithing.

Many people have adopted an attitude that tithing is something they have to put up with and get out of the way each week. They see it as a duty to check off of their Sunday to-do list. Other people have gone the opposite direction, imbuing the tithe with a supernatural quick-fix magic quality that God never intended it to have. Both of these approaches are equally wrong. They warp what the Bible teaches about the tithe and deny Christians of the rich blessings that God has in store for us if only we will approach the tithe His way.

The Heart of a Tither

There is a vast difference between *bringing the tithe* and *being a tither*. Let me say that another way: Just because you tithe every Sunday does not mean you're a tither! In their book *Wealth, Riches & Money, God's Biblical Principles of Finance*, Craig Hill and Earl Pitts put it in a nutshell: "Many people are tithing but never become tithers."[2] That's true, because the issue is one of intensity of heart. "The difference has to do with the attitude and active involvement,"[3] write Hill and Pitts. For example, you might love to play football at the park now and then, but that doesn't make you an Emmit Smith or a David Beckham. You might love to play tennis on occasion, but that doesn't make you a Steffi Graf or a Venus or Vanessa Williams. A professional athlete has devotion, dedication and passion about his or her sport, which presses him or her to be great. A true tither will have the drive, desire and commitment of a pro.

God doesn't want our money. He wants our hearts. Tithers bring a heart after God. The woman in Mark 12 and Luke 21, who gave the two mites, was blessed by Jesus because she had a heart that told her that it *all* belonged to the Lord. Two mites may not have been much by the standards of other people, but it was a massive amount to her—and she earmarked 100 percent for God! It was all she had to live on, and she was blessed by Jesus because her heart prompted her to give her all:

> [Jesus] looked up and saw the rich putting their gifts into the treasury, and He saw also a certain poor widow putting in two mites. So He said, "Truly I say to you that this poor widow has put in more than all; for all these out of their abundance have put in offerings for God, but she out of her poverty put in all the livelihood that she had" (Luke 21:1-4).

Cain and Abel: A Lesson in Tithing

To further demonstrate the heart of a tither, to faithfully bring the tithe and to do so with the best intentions, let's look at the story of Cain and Abel.

> And in the process of time it came to pass that Cain brought an offering of the fruit of the ground to the LORD. Abel also brought of the firstborn of his flock and of their fat. And the LORD respected Abel and his offering, but He did not respect Cain and his offering. And Cain was very angry, and his countenance fell. So the LORD said to Cain, "Why are you angry? And why has your countenance fallen? If you do well, will you not be accepted? And if you do not do well, sin lies at the door. And its desire is for you, but you should rule over it" (Gen.4:3-7).

Cain and Abel were brothers who both brought offerings to God. Cain brought "of the fruit of the ground" (a crop offering) and Abel brought of his livestock. People often interpret this text as saying that the reason Cain's offering was not accepted was because he did not bring a blood offering but brought of his crops, whereas Abel brought of a blood offering from his animals. I disagree with that interpretation.

Here's why: There are ample times in the Bible when God affirms tithes of crops or harvest, particularly in an agrarian society. Whatever a culture values, accepts and barters with as a medium of exchange for goods and services is acceptable as a tithe and offering. The tithe is given in the context of the medium of exchange for a culture, and every culture has various mediums of exchange. The exchange of harvest or crops was as legitimate back then as the exchange of livestock. For example, farmers and ranchers both brought offerings out of the increase within their individual professions. One, a farmer, raising and dealing in crops. The other, a rancher, raising and dealing in livestock. Thus, it was not the substance of Cain's offering that was in question; *it was his attitude*.

My son, Kendan, who is in culinary school, taught my wife and me about the different parts of an animal having varying degrees of value. Some parts are more valuable than others. Abel's tithe was honored because he brought of the "firstlings" of his flock *and* of "the fat thereof." The fat was the most valuable part of the animal. "The fat thereof" means that Abel *went over and above* and prepared and brought to God the most precious part of the animal. He could have simply brought the standard sacrificial animal, but he went beyond that minimum requirement, because of his heart for God. The difference in the two men was not so much in the offering as it was in his *attitude* before and after the offering.

There were two problems with Cain's offering: First, Genesis 4:3 says, "*in the process of time it came to pass*, that Cain brought of the fruit of the ground an offering unto the LORD" (emphasis added). "In the process of time" indicates that Cain brought his sacrifice *after a while*—the phrase indicates *lingering time*. In other words, Cain brought his sacrifice when he got around to it. Problem number one! Can you imagine keeping God waiting for what is His?

Then, Genesis 4:4 says that the Lord respected, or received, Abel's offering, but He did not receive Cain's. When his late, mediocre offering was not accepted, what did Cain do? He got ticked off! Cain became angry and "his countenance fell." Basically, he copped an attitude. He became upset.

I love how God responded to that. The Lord said to Cain, "Why are you angry, and why is your countenance fallen?" In effect, God was saying, "What's wrong with you? Why are you so upset?" God continued in verse 7, "If thou doest well," which is a phrase meaning *if you adjust your attitude*. Basically, "What's wrong with you? If you would have had an attitude check, you would have stepped up your offering and yours would have been accepted, too."

Check It Before You Wreck It

Let each one give as he purposes in his heart, not grudgingly or of necessity; for God loves a cheerful giver.

2 Corinthians 9:7

The lesson in the account of the offering of Cain and Abel is not in the substance of the offering—it is in the attitude behind the offerings. Cain and Abel both brought an offering, but each had a different attitude. This indicates the difference between a person who brings the tithe and a person who is a tither. That difference is *attitude*—how we respond in our heart to what we bring to the Lord. The one who simply brings the tithe is bringing the right amount with the wrong attitude.

God is not merely looking for His tenth. God wants to move us beyond a restrictive, stale, legalistic mind-set that keeps tabs on precise numbers, and get us closer to Him, into a realm where we can breathe His air of carefree faith!

When it's time for the offering in the midst of a service, how do you feel? Do you twinge inside, or does your heart leap? What kind of attitude shift do you make when it's time to put your offering in that plate? Do you slip out the back door just before the tithe is taken? Do you arrive just late enough to miss the offering? How often does the tithe call cause you to shout?

If you want a closer walk with the Lord, if you want to grow in ways that please Him, then take a hard look at your attitude. Paul makes a powerful statement about attitude in giving. He encourages those of us who gather to worship but for one reason or another have nothing to offer. God never expects you to give what you don't have (see 2 Cor. 8:12) and He knows what you have and whether or not you can afford to give. After all, everything you have, He gave you. He is always more concerned about the attitude of your heart when giving. Paul says the Lord seeks a mind that is willing to give, and that God values willingness far beyond the amount on the check. The principle of the tithe is not the legislation of law, but the demonstration of a heart that places God first. For the willing heart, the tithe is not a matter of legalism, but realism. It is part of your "reasonable worship" (see Rom. 12:1). And it just makes sense! If God is in fact first in your life, why *wouldn't* you tithe?

Ask yourself why giving at 10 percent is not fair to God. If you are honest, whatever answer you give will most likely be the result of selfishness, pride or lack of understanding the principle of the tithe. (Hopefully, this book is helping to eliminate that last option!)

The Curse from Disobedience

Deuteronomy 28 says that if we're not careful to do as God says, we're in big trouble:

> But it shall come to pass, if you do not obey the voice of the LORD your God, to observe carefully all His commandments and His statutes which I command you today, that all these curses will come upon you and overtake you (v. 15).

The text goes on to list some pretty horrid curses that will befall Israel if they are disobedient and step out from under the protection and guidance of the Lord:

> Cursed shall you be in the city, and cursed shall you be in the country. Cursed shall be your basket and your kneading bowl. Cursed shall be the fruit of your body and the produce of your land, the increase of your cattle and the offspring of your flocks. Cursed shall you be when you come in, and cursed shall you be when you go out (vv. 16-19).

Our finances can be drastically affected as a result of our disobedience. This passage talks about the fact that disobedience makes us prey for a world system that is influenced by the spirit of mammon. Not only do the disobedient fall prey to it, but they also become slaves to it, because they fall into bondage to whatever other source they choose to follow.

God's Perpetual Circle of Giving

He who sows sparingly will also reap sparingly, and he who sows bountifully will also reap bountifully.

2 Corinthians 9:6

What seems like a parallel in the verse above is actually not. He who gives sparingly shall reap sparingly—true. However, "he who sows bountifully" has a different meaning than simply he who gives more. It sounds like the text is implying that when we give a little we get a little, and when we give a lot we get a lot in return. But that's not what it means. Remember, it's not about *amount*. What the text is saying is that if you sow as a miser or a penny pincher or a cheapskate, the result will be commensurate blessings of *type* and *substance*—not necessarily of amount.

The word "bountifully" (*eulogia*, in Greek) is another form of the word for "blessing." He who gives or sows as a blessing to someone or something shall receive blessings because he gave as a blessing. Picture it as a perpetual circle of escalating giving and receiving: God gives us the grace to give. When we give, God releases favor. That which we give activates more grace in our lives, which then activates our hearts to give even more, which then spurs God to respond even more.

Remember, God's covenant with us is to bless us and make us a blessing to others. He blesses us by giving us the ability to gain the wealth. That wealth establishes God's covenant with us (which, again, is to bless us and flow blessings through us as we follow Him).

Here is what the Perpetual Circle of God's Grace looks like in diagram:

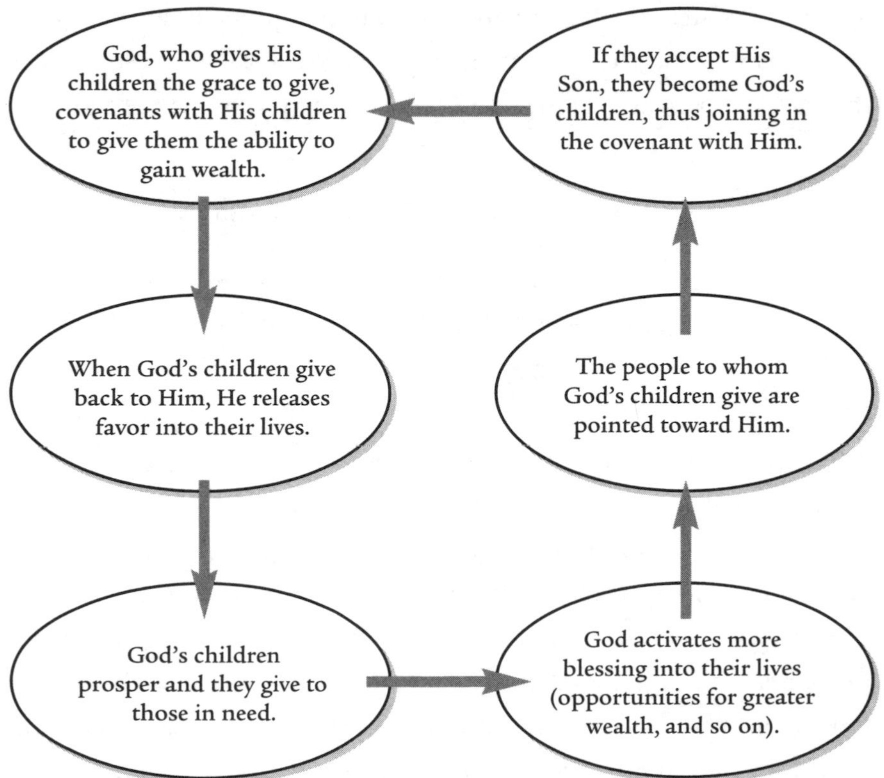

Notice that it's all a circular relationship between us and God, and goes round and round like an engine, with God as the Power that gets the engine going, which then feeds the energy (His power) back to us, and we gain wealth, which we give to others, who are pointed toward God, who gives them the grace to give once they accept His Son (thus "powering up" their relationship with God), and on and on.

A Caveat

God says that if we tithe, He will open for us the windows of heaven and pour out such blessing that there will not be room enough to receive it, and He will rebuke the devourer for our sakes so that he will not destroy (see Mal. 3:10-11).

This does not necessarily mean that He'll pour out a new car. He might not pour out cash. Maybe not a free house. Now, none of those are impossible for God to do—however, the text says He'll pour out a "blessing." That blessing is the ability—the power—to gain wealth. What this means, according to Malachi 3, is that when we take God at His own word and we tithe, He will open up the windows of heaven and give us such an amount of blessing (the ability to gain wealth) that it will be above and beyond our imagination to have conceived it.

It Is Holy

One of the reasons many people don't know how to handle money wisely is because they don't know how to handle their own lives wisely. In Leviticus 11:44, God says, "You shall be holy; for I am holy." That's not a suggestion—it's a command. Without holiness, we won't even come close to seeing God—no matter what denomination we belong to, no matter what church we attend. Our life is to be set apart and holy. We live and breathe at the pleasure of God. Holiness is a declaration that we belong to Him.

This is an all-encompassing call. Being holy applies to all realms of our lives—marriage, money, relationships, jobs, everything. Only once we have this straight and working properly can we "set apart" our money to God with the right attitude.

This set-apart holiness is similar to a home purchase. If you are in the process of buying a house, there is an escrow account into which you deposit money. That money can be used for that purpose only. It is consecrated, dedicated to just one thing: the house. *Period.* You declare that money to be holy—set apart—because it is now off limits to you. It doesn't matter if the baby needs new shoes. It doesn't matter if the credit card company finally found you. It doesn't matter if you see the repo man driving past your front window in what used to be your car. You cannot go and take that escrow money and handle it as though it's yours, because once it's in the escrow account, it is set aside for that house only. It is to your benefit, but the bank controls it. If you somehow manage to get into that account and take a little money from it and go down to Macy's and spend it on yourself, then you have taken money that was set aside for one purpose and have used it for your own personal benefit. And you might be in danger of losing your house, because that money was dedicated and devoted to one thing.

It's the same with God. He says that when you mess with what belongs to Him and you desecrate His escrow account or when you fail to make the deposits into it, you become the perfect candidate for missing out on a blessing, and your whole family will suffer for it.

The tithe is a kind of escrow for your treasures-in-heaven account. When you fail to dedicate the tithe as holy, then you have chosen to take that which is under God's control. That money is accruing to your benefit, because when the deal closes, you have a blessing waiting for you: a new house! You don't want to jeopardize that.

Compromise on your tithes and you compromise your blessings.

Cause and Effect

After we give our tithe, that first-fruit makes everything after that holy. For example, Jesus was the first-born of God—that made what follows Jesus as holy. Likewise, our tithing, our first-fruits right off the top of what first comes into our household, makes the rest of our money "holy," or blessed by God, so that the remaining 90 percent is holy unto God—it is sanctified to bless us. In other words, when you sanctify the first to God, the rest is blessed to you.

However, if we don't sanctify (that is, give the tithe), the rest can't be blessed and it can't grow and multiply. When we desecrate that which belongs to God, He says, *Fine—then you will not stand against your enemy.* We become vulnerable to the attack of the devil when we withhold what is the Lord's.

God says, *Let there be an attitude check. Bring the tithe and see if I won't open the windows of heaven and really bless you.* When we do try Him and tithe regularly, it gives God an opportunity to prove Himself to us and make a liar out of the devil. It builds faith. It banishes fear. It blesses finances. The promises of the tithe are *powerful*!

A Principle of Priority

Second Corinthians 9:7 says that God loves a particular kind of giver: the kind who gives cheerfully! Our hearts determine how we give, because we tend to give as an expression of that which we treasure. "God loves a cheerful giver" indicates that cheerful giving catches God's eye, and He then "is able to make all grace abound toward you" (2 Cor. 9:8). The phrase speaks of God's volition, His determined will. God *wills* to increase, to multiply, the seed. He *wills* to bless us and release grace to us when we display a right attitude in giving.

If you are leery about the topic of tithing, make a choice to simply *trust God*. It's amazing how the Holy Spirit lifts. Let that day come when you go beyond clap-and-song offerings to the Lord. One day God is going to push the replay button on your life and give you a flashback. He will bring into your mind all that He carried you through. How He has blessed you. How He has been faithful to you. How He put food on your table when you didn't have the money. How you paid bills with an empty checking account He put money into that you never saw coming. How He brought people into your life at just the right time with just the right gift when you needed it most.

How we give is governed by our hearts. "Let each one give as he purposes in his heart" (2 Cor. 9:7) shows that the act of giving surpasses *amount* and deals with the *attitude* that precipitated the amount.

I'll say it again: God does not need your money—He wants your heart, for where your treasure is, your heart will follow. And if He has your heart—if *He* is your treasure—then you will follow Him. Hopefully you are beginning to see that tithing is about more than money. It is a principle of priority. It is a spiritual practice that demonstrates the preeminence of God in your life. It is an acknowledgment that you live your life in relationship to a Higher Authority and a higher principle, which is to receive and release blessings as you honor the God who is the Source of your ability to gain an income and make a living.

Don't let anyone quench your spirit when it's time to give. You know how good God has been to you. Isn't He worth the 10 percent He asks of you?

Notes

1. This means that God's gift of salvation is not just for the "circumcision" (the Jews), because Abraham was uncircumcised when God made the promise of the covenant with him. This makes the covenant transdispensational. In other words, it applies to gentiles (the "uncircumcision"), as well.
2. Craig Hill and Earl Pitts, *Wealth, Riches and Money, God's Biblical Principles of Finance* (Atlaspark, South Africa: Ruach Communications), p. 126.
3. Ibid.

Section II

Undoing What Has Been Done

Oscar Wilde once wrote, "Experience is the name everyone gives to their mistakes."[1] Once we make a mistake, we must learn from the experience and resolve not to repeat it. Every adult in the world can attest to the fact that life is full of making mistakes—and hopefully learn from them. The same holds true for the Church. There are certain errors and mistaken mind-sets that even Christians are prone to make.

In this section we will examine three common mistakes many churches perpetuate: (1) removing process from prosperity; (2) buying the poverty lie; and (3) perpetuating the curse of financial bondage.

Note

1. Oscar Wilde (1854–1900), *Lady Windermere's Fan,* Act II (1892).

Chapter 7

Putting Process Back into Prosperity

Due to some extremist theological positions that have distorted biblical truth about prosperity, many people have simply tossed the subject out altogether and don't want to hear about it anymore. That is a trick of the enemy that causes many to miss out on the blessings God means for them.

There is a dangerous credulity in the Body of Christ. "Credulity" is belief without inspection: Because Prophet So-and-So with the pink suit and gold chains said it, then people believe it. The problem is that what the good prophet said often does not agree with the Word of God. I can hear the Lord saying, "I have not sent these prophets, yet they ran; I have not spoken to them, yet they prophesied" (Jer. 23:21). Prosperity is not about a touch, a falling out or a slap on the forehead. It's about *God's process.*

There is nothing negative about prosperity. In fact, prosperity is a biblical precept that means "to thrive economically." The misunderstanding arises when preachers strip God's process from the topic of achieving prosperity and teach only a partial and fractured gospel on this important subject.

The Partial-Gospel Problem

Healing, deliverance, prosperity—none of these simply lands in our laps. They all require a specific biblical process, and many churches overlook that reality.

The Bible says God *pours out* blessings (see Mal. 3:10). Sometimes a blessing is simply giving you enough sense to get out of bed and get to work! God has given each of us the power and ability to accomplish, but *we* have to do it. God opened up the windows of heaven and got you a job; now you've got to get to it and make something of it. Dollar cakes don't rain on us like manna from heaven. Too many saints plant themselves on the sidelines, waiting for a super-miracle to float down from heaven after somebody lays hands on them, pats them on the head, and shouts, "Be prosperous, hallelujah!"

This incomplete teaching is being taught under the cloak of spirituality. People go to prosperity conventions and wave hands and shout "Shebaba!" and throw "anointed" handkerchiefs—and they're still broke! For the most part, these people tend to be "gimme-gimme anointing junkies" who go all over the country to get somebody else's anointing.

God does want to bless us, but He wants to bless us through the rarely spoken-of dynamic of the Christian life called *laboring*! We are *laborers*. Servants of the King. Not many people want to hear much about *work*, but the truth is, we get our anointing by *doing* as God instructs.

The so-called "prosperity message" is often presented in a way that implies that if we follow steps one, two and three, then when we wake up tomorrow, somebody will touch us on the shoulder and *bang!*—we'll have it all.

"Do you want to be a millionaire?!"

"Yes!"

"Is that your final answer?!"

"Yes, yes! Right now!"

But what makes me think that just because I'm a Christian I'm ready to handle millions of dollars God's way right now? What makes me think that God thinks I'm ready? What makes me think that I wouldn't squander it all, due to my not having gone through the process of building, learning and growing? Jesus never said we can have it our way, right away—nowhere does the Bible teach that.

Laboring means that God will do His part, but we've got to do our part as well. And our part is not standing in the healing line and the blessing line and the prosperity line and the anointing line, pulling some lever to get a morsel of blessing. Our job is to properly handle what we've got, and to get involved with business and financial affairs and investments in a manner that honors God. We are partners in a process.

You Can't Microwave Your Blessing!

They thought the kingdom of God would appear immediately.

LUKE 19:11

Jesus spoke the parable of the minas in a particular context during a time when the disciples were expecting the Kingdom to be established immediately. The Church of today has bought into that same *gotta-have-it-now* mentality and is attempting to transfer it to the mind-set of the Master. This contradicts the exhortation of Romans 12:2: "Do not be conformed to this world, but be transformed by the renewing of your mind." We cannot approach our relationship with God as if He's a vending machine, as if we can press a button and get what we want from Him immediately.

When I was a little boy and we would go to Monday night prayer meetings, I remember the deacons praying, "Right now, Lord! *Right now!* Do it *now*, Lord! Hallelujah thank You in the name of Jeeeezus!" Did they ever pray that at your church? *Right now, Lord!* Then we'd come back the next week and the preacher would have to pray the very same thing all over again because God didn't do the right now right then. "Right now, *one more time*, Lord!" The *right now, Lord* didn't happen, because God is not our bellhop.

This points out another problem with the incomplete teaching on handling money properly: It paints God as our servant, a *gofer* who we send to "go-fer this" and "go-fer that." But we don't ring our spiritual bell and cause God to jump to attention. Rather, He is looking for willing hearts that say, "Right now, Lord, I am ready to do what *You* want me to do!"

We cannot microwave spirituality. There is no fast track to maturity any more than there's a quick way for children to grow up (contrary to what they may think!). No one achieves instant maturity. There is no formula, no potion, no magic words, no holy glance that makes us instantly mature. The bottom line is, we've got to *go through* something in order to *know* something, and we've got to *know* something in order to *be* something. That is a *process*, and processes take time.

Proclaiming a gospel that removes process prevents process. That, in turn, causes us to feel that Jesus' coming must be *soon*, our child's healing is going to come *immediately*, we have to achieve financial security *right now*. However, focusing on episodes of instantaneous healing overlooks God's sovereignty, distorts theology and moves people into a false mind-set that alters their relationship with God and shifts them into the non-biblical, gotta-have-it-now attitude of the world.

Thought Creates

Do not be conformed to this world, but be transformed by the renewing of your mind, *that you may prove what is that good and acceptable and perfect will of God.*

ROMANS 12:2, EMPHASIS ADDED

Once we learn and understand God's purposes for money, it is important to begin walking in those purposes and instilling and integrating that understanding into our thinking process—to "renew our mind," as Paul puts it in Romans 12:2.

For example, how much of your last paycheck brought forth a profit? Most people know how much they gave toward the church offering, how much they'll need for the rent or mortgage, approximately how much groceries will cost each week, how much money it takes to maintain their household from month to month, and so forth. Each of those monthly debit amounts is important to know. But how much of the money from your last paycheck actually *produced* something, *built* something, *created* something? In other words, how much of your income *returned a profit* on itself?

It's time to begin thinking differently. Your work may have stopped when you left your workplace and deposited your paycheck in the bank, but that shouldn't stop your money from working. Thought is the genesis of new creation. Begin to think differently and you will soon behave differently. Begin to behave differently than in the past and you will soon *be* different. One of the first steps in training yourself to think differently is to learn to speak affirmatively—out loud. Train yourself to make positive declarations from your lips. These vocal affirmations will soon begin to sink deeply into your spirit. These thoughts will become part of you. They will *become* you. Why? Because *thought creates.*

If God puts the thought in your mind and you have the Holy Spirit in your heart, and the examples of Jesus are guiding your steps, what can hinder you? I don't care what age you are. I don't care what position you are in life. I don't care about your height or your weight or your skin color, tone or texture. Speak proactive declarations, repeat them to yourself aloud, get them into your spirit—and then *act on them*! I don't care if you're in school or whether you own a business. I don't care if you're at the top of a corporate ladder or if you're on your way up. I don't care if you're single or married. Open your mouth and make a firm declaration in faith under God. Get this thinking into your spirit.

If you can ever understand the dimensions of our mighty God, it will vastly enlarge the dimensions of your dreams. Many Christians haven't understood that yet—and they have God on their side! You can't expand a kingdom without the resources to do so. And the process of accumulating the necessary financial resources to expand the kingdom begins with commerce, with business and with wise money management.

Once you get the simple truth into your mind that God is leading every step you take with Him, and once you begin to make an honest, consistent effort to take care of business God's way and make your money count for His kingdom, then you will be actively involved in expanding God's kingdom on Earth with the material increase that He will entrust into your care.

One of the lessons of the parable of Luke 19 is that something tangible and life-changing is going to happen in the future, and in order to get ready for the future, we've got to do something *now*—today. What happened in the servants' future was huge: Their master returned, conducted an accounting of their business activities, passed judgment and bestowed massive rewards and crushing punishment. There was no excuse. They were told to do something in preparation for his return.

It is important that we get it into our mind that it's about tomorrow, next year, the time to come, the future, and we must be preparing for then *right now*. It will be here sooner than you think.

The Meantime Season

One of the biggest problems people face in their relationship with God today has to do with *the meantime*. As we learned, nearly 2,000 years ago, Jesus realized that His disciples were anticipating that God's kingdom on Earth had arrived, that Jesus was going to establish His kingdom right then and there. Jesus addressed their misperception by teaching them the parable of the minas, which said in essence that the King is coming but not right away. There will be a delay in His coming. And in the meantime, the people of God have a responsibility to perform a *specific duty*.

When our spirits and our minds tell us God is coming, we find ourselves asking in the flesh, "but when?" We find ourselves wanting and expecting God to move immediately, often because we feel we need it right now. But God does not always work that way. He's too big to jump when we say, "jump!" He sticks to His plan. He follows His *process*. Remember the parable of the minas and the nobleman: The master said there would be a delay in his coming, *but he did come.* So will Jesus.

The good news about the "meantime" is that we're not left to our own devices. God gives us resources with which to do our job. Paul says in 2 Corinthians 9:10 that God gives us "seed." What do you do with the seed? You don't eat the seed; you sow it. When the seed brings forth a crop, you eat some of the crop, but not all of it. Why? Because the crop also contains seed for future crops, and if you eat all of your seed, there won't be anything left to multiply.

Prosperity, growth and achievement don't happen instantly. You don't plant a seed in the ground, add a little water and *boom!* it becomes a bush. It takes time. The master put the money into his servants' care, along with instructions for what they were to do with the money, and then he went away. And it was during that time period when they put the money to work that it increased. It was all part of a process—a process that we must put back into prosperity.

Chapter 8

Poverty Is No Virtue

The plans of the diligent lead surely to plenty,
but those of everyone who is hasty, surely to poverty.

Proverbs 21:5

As we learned in the previous chapter, the fulfillment of the promises of God involves a process. It is still true that patience is a virtue; however, some people actually believe that poverty is a sign of virtue or holiness or piety. *Wrong.*

The idea that poverty is somehow a mark of spirituality is a lie the devil uses to mislead Christians. The Bible speaks nearly four times as often about prospering than it does about poverty. Since prospering appears more often in God's Word than poverty does, then we too should give it more attention, in order to better understand what God says concerning this subject, and to be wary of the schemes of the enemy who is trying to rob us of what God wants for us.

The Bible warns *against* a mind-set that leads to poverty, even identifying it as shameful—and sometimes even a consequence of sin. Let's start with a quick look at God's Word pertaining to poverty, from Proverbs, the book of wisdom:

> A little sleep, a little slumber, a little folding of the hands to rest—and poverty will come on you like a bandit and scarcity like an armed man (6:10-11; 24:33-34, *NIV*).

> Poverty is the ruin of the poor (10:15, *NIV*).
>
> One man gives freely, yet gains even more; another withholds unduly, but comes to poverty (11:24, *NIV*).
>
> Poverty and shame will come to him who disdains correction (13:18).
>
> In all labor there is profit, but idle chatter leads only to poverty (14:23).
>
> Do not love sleep, lest you come to poverty (20:13).
>
> The plans of the diligent lead to profit as surely as haste leads to poverty (21:5, *NIV*).
>
> The drunkard and the glutton will come to poverty (23:21).
>
> A stingy man is eager to get rich and is unaware that poverty awaits him (28:22, *NIV*).

As the above verses indicate, the Bible speaks *against* an attitude that leads to poverty—actions and inactions that can lead to poverty—and these examples come from just one book of the Bible! Nowhere in Scripture is poverty identified as lofty. There is nothing "holy" or spiritual about lack.

The Problem with Poverty

One problem with poverty is that when we're experiencing it, we can't give financially to benefit God's kingdom, because we're constantly struggling to be financial receivers for our basic sustenance.

One of the ways the enemy will attack us in how we handle our money is to try to get us over our head in debt. If all of your resources are going to pay debt, then you have nothing to bless anybody with—which is exactly what the enemy wants. He wants you to struggle through life, never quite making ends meet and never being able to help anyone in need. But that's not what God wants for you. His intention is for us to have abundant provisions and to be a blessing to others.

I cannot tell you the number of people who have come to me with tears in their eyes, saying, "Pastor, you know I really wish I could give to this ministry and that fund, but I just can't afford it right now." If there is a cause for the Kingdom that you cannot afford to give to, then you've messed up somewhere and you've got to do whatever it takes to set it straight. If you have dug yourself into a hole, the first thing you've got to do is *start digging*. Dig yourself out so that you can be a positive testimony and so that you can contribute to Kingdom causes. The Bible says that God gives us all the things that we have *as supply toward the work of the Kingdom*. If you don't have it, it's because you went off of God's path in some way. But don't drop your head and mope about it, just get your act together! Jesus hasn't returned yet. Pay your bills. Take care of business. Get back in the game!

Most of the people I know aren't in trouble because they have no money—they're in trouble because they've mishandled the money they have. It isn't that God hasn't blessed them; it's that they haven't wisely used what He blessed them with. Remember, it's not how much money you get; it's *how you handle* what you get.

It breaks my heart to see people who love the Lord but are unable to sow into the Kingdom because they have not been faithful with the money and material blessings God has given them. If you're worried about how you're going to make ends meet and you've got bill collectors coming after you and you are running out of money before you run out of month, something is seriously wrong! That is *not* God's way for you.

I know. I've been there. I've done that. You're not alone. Along about the nineteenth and twentieth of the month, I was getting into big trouble. It was not peaceful. I felt like I was stuck in some kind of terrible cycle. I'd get a headache every 20 days or so, and it was because I couldn't pay my bills. My wife and I were messed up! So I went to the Word, studied what God has to say on the subject, and learned about this process for how to make my money count, instead of always having to count my money.

Encourage Others

Encourage others to break old patterns and to start being responsible with their money, too. If there are people who owe you money to whom you've said, "Just pay me back whenever you can," then you have just preached a poverty mind-set to that person by encouraging her to remain in debt and basically giving her permission to be irresponsible. When you take out a loan at a bank, they don't tell you, "Baby, just pray to Jesus and pay us when you get it." You deflect spiritual growth when a person owes you money but you don't hold him accountable to repay you.

When you loan money on the "pay when you can" basis, chances are you aren't going to get your money back anyway. It doesn't matter how much you love Jesus and are on your way to heaven, just kiss it goodbye because you probably won't ever see that money again—and that person will move on to his next freebie loan, having learned nothing. Either give the money as a gift or set a clear repayment schedule—but if you can't stand to lose it, don't loan it. Help your brothers and sisters in the Lord by keeping them fiscally accountable.

Break the Cycle

Poverty is destitution—a state of *lack*. There is nothing spiritual about poverty. My friend comedian Steve Harvey often says, "The best thing you can do for poor people is not be one of them!" Steve's point is that the poor can't help the poor. If you're in poverty, break the cycle now. Get out of debt so that you can be a contributor to the Kingdom, so that you can live in God's blessings. Our God is a giving God who is wealthy beyond measure, as it says in 1 Chronicles: "Both riches and honor come from You" (29:12).

A paycheck is money you work for. Riches are money that *works for you*. Riches take you into the area of overflow. Riches have to do with what you have after you've paid all your bills and met your obligations and needs. Riches have to do with expendable resources that go beyond your needs. Riches are when your money does the work. *That* is God's desire for His children. Maybe God's will for your financial life begins with you getting out of debt and your no longer being in slavery to bills and creditors. For you, the issue may not be how much money you make or even how much money you give, but whether you are handling whatever you do have in a manner that honors God by making Him first in your finances.

Our God is rich beyond measure. Clearly, poverty is no virtue. But wealth in the hands of the wise works wonders!

CHAPTER 9

Bondage Versus Freedom: The Seven Indicators

I am concerned for the church because there are many Christians out there who are in financial bondage and have fallen under the curse of fiscal slavery. God is clear that this is not His way. He wants us free of debt and oppressive monetary burden.

If you're in financial bondage, there's nothing to be ashamed of. You just need to get out of it. The first step is to determine if and how you're in bondage. The following seven indicators will help you ascertain whether or not you're in financial bondage:

Indicator 1:

You Have More Faith in Material Goods than You Do in God

You say, "I am rich, have become wealthy, and have need of nothing"—
and do not know that you are wretched, miserable, poor, blind, and naked.

REVELATION 3:17

As the Scripture above indicates, the people in the church in the wealthy city of Laodicea thought they didn't need God. Although they were Christians, they had become smug and self-sufficient, trusting in their wealth more than in their God and putting their faith in material possessions.

If you ever find yourself thinking, *Wow! Look what I've managed to accumulate all on my own*, beware! To that, God replies, "I hate pride and arrogance. Pride goes before destruction, and a haughty spirit before a fall" (see Prov. 8:13). Trusting in material things (which fade away, gather rust, collect moths and disappear) is like trusting in a boat with a rotting hull. Eventually, the bottom is going to drop out. When you think about it, we actually have nothing apart from God.

> Do not lay up for yourselves treasures on earth, where moth and rust destroy and where thieves break in and steal; but lay up for yourselves treasures in Heaven, where neither moth nor rust destroys and where thieves do not break in and steal (Matt. 6:19-20).

In Revelation 3, God warns the Laodicean Christians to repent. He says, "As many as I love, I rebuke and chasten. Therefore be zealous and repent" (v. 19). If you are trusting in your material goods more than God, repent! He rebukes and chastens us because He loves us and He knows there are more secure and profitable ways to follow.

Indicator 2:

You Place Your Material Desires and Motives Above Your Desire for God

Is what you want more important to you than what God wants for you? Do you seek His guidance and wisdom before you make larger than normal monetary expenditures? When you place your own desires above God's desires and you start thinking, "I see what I want and I'm going to get it no matter what. I've got the money to buy it, I have my credit card, I have my cash and I'm going to buy it," then you're in bondage! What if God doesn't want you to have it? What if He has a way in mind that is much better? Have you gone so far into bondage that you've painted yourself into a corner far from His path?

Indicator 3:
You Have a Burning Desire to Get Rich Quick

Proverbs 28:20 says, "He who hastens to be rich will not go unpunished." To try to get rich quickly—to "hasten to get rich"—is not of God. For example, trying to get rich quick through playing the lottery or gambling is not of God. That is bondage. It doesn't matter if you're wealthy or poor—if you're "hastening to be rich," it's all the same: You're in bondage.

Indicator 4:
You Have to Delay Paying Your Monthly Bills

If you are always behind in paying your bills, you are in bondage. The Bible warns us, "Do not say to your neighbor, 'Go, and come back, and tomorrow I will give it,' when you have it with you" (Prov. 3:28). In other words, don't say you're going to pay on time and then not follow through.

When you owe somebody something and you don't repay them when you promised (or don't pay at all!), that's a poor advertisement for godly living. How can you tell people about Jesus and how He will supply all of their needs when you yourself aren't living with God as your need-meeter? Pay off your debt! The person you're trying to witness to doesn't want your Jesus; he wants the money you owe him!

Indicator 5:
You Compromise Your Christian Ethics

When some people who owe money start getting collection calls, they actually lie, or change their phone number, or get a post office box or change their address—all in an effort to avoid their creditors! Where in the Bible are we advised to deceive, cheat and steal? When people go to great lengths to *not pay* what they legitimately owe, that's stealing, plain and simple. It compromises Christian ethics.

And it's a sign like a boulevard billboard that screams out, "I'm in bondage!"

Morals, ethics and godly living are a testimony to those around us. Don't compromise. If you're willing to compromise, you're willing to bend. When you're willing to bend, you're ready to break. When you're ready to break—you have arrived at the devil's door.

Indicator 6:

You Fail to Make Investments and Save for Future Needs

You are in bondage when you fail to make preparations for the future by saving and investing with an eye toward future needs. To that I say, "Go to the ant, you sluggard; consider its ways and be wise!" (Prov. 6:6).

The ant is a smart little insect. It is always planning and working ahead. I have never seen a lazy ant, sitting on its haunches, taking a break. They are always hauling food, building anthills and scouting out new supply sources. Ants are always on the go, *go, Go!* They work ahead to store up for future needs. Nobody taught them to do it; it's just their natural instinct to know they're going to need it. If an ant can do that, can't you? You're smarter than an ant.

You need to have at least three to six months of income saved up as a safety net. If you don't, you're in danger of falling into financial bondage.

Indicator 7:

A Man Forces His Wife to Work

I will run the risk of being labeled old-fashioned on this one. I want to raise some issues that I hope will prompt you to look at some things from a little different perspective. Here it is: If a man puts his wife to work to help pay the bills, he's in bondage. If your wife works just because you need her income to make ends meet, it might be that you are either living beyond your needs or you've been financially unwise. That puts you in bondage. A wife should only work if she wants to. She should not *have* to work.

Many Christian couples in today's society have allowed themselves to be convinced that it is necessary for two people to work in order to make ends meet. People have gotten so greedy and affected by the standards of the culture—keeping up with the Joneses—that they don't want to humble themselves enough to live in an apartment while saving up for a real estate investment in the future. Instead, they jump into a house they can't really afford. Instead of driving the used Chevy they can afford, they hustle up a down payment for a new BMW—and can't even afford the gas and upkeep for it. Their solution becomes demanding that the wife go to work.

Let me hasten to clarify that I advocate this position only in cases where there are young children in the home. I probably should say, "You are in bondage if your wife is a mother and you force her to go to work." This indicator of financial bondage is also related to our priorities and your material desires and motives. In no way is my intention to devalue the incredible gifts, talents, academic achievement and professional savvy of women who are also mothers. My point (and this may get me into trouble with some readers!) is that the basic responsibility for the financial stability of the family rests squarely with the husband.

Wherever possible, I believe the financial foundation of the home is the man's responsibility, and that the wife's income should be an optional choice the couple makes in light of the priority of the care for their children. I am by no means speaking dogmatically. I am not talking about those rough years where a husband is in school and the loving wife carries the financial load. I am not talking about those seasons of illness, immobility or other unexpected, uncontrollable circumstances that all couples sometimes face in life. I am lifting up a principle. I am putting forth the point that the basic responsibilities for the financial foundation of the home ought to be covered whenever possible by the husband—and, ideally, that the income of the wife is the family's "financial gravy."

I am focusing particularly on the household that includes children. I have spoken with many good mothers who struggle with self-image and fulfillment because they are in such financial bondage that they have to work, and their job responsibilities cause great frustration because they are not able to be home with her children—especially during the tender, formative years. The desire of a mother's heart is to be at home instead of in the boardroom, at the computer or at a desk.

On the other hand, I know of many couples that have to make the often painful decision to delay having children because they literally can't afford for the wife to stop working and start the family they both want. Time and time again they express their grief over financial choices and misplaced priorities that have thrust them into financial bondage. The industrious woman in Proverbs 31 is as gifted as her male counterpart, but she seems to have learned to balance her industrious professional life with the intimate domestic life with her children and family. When she is forced to choose between a paycheck and her tender care for her children on a level that *only she* can provide, that marriage is in financial bondage. When she has to choose between hearing a boss give her another assignment on her job and hearing a babysitter tell her about the baby's first step or a new word her child has said, that marriage is in financial bondage.

This isn't to say your wife can't work to bring in some income above and beyond that which goes toward the basic necessities. But to rely on her to help provide for the essentials, the necessities, is not God's way. The man is responsible for the basic needs of the family. He is to "nourish and cherish" his wife and be the provider. If the family is in a financial quandary, the man is accountable for straightening it out.

It's just amazing to me how many men want to be the head of the family, the one in charge, the boss, yet often they don't want to take care of all the responsibilities that come with that position. My brothers, if you want to be the head, then be so in *every* way. You can't pick and choose.

And, ladies, if a man can't take care of himself before he marries you, what makes you think he'll be able to *after* you marry him? Before you get married, watch to see how he handles his own responsibilities, because he'll bring those same habits into the marriage. "Husbands ought to love their own wives as their own bodies; he who loves his wife loves himself" (Eph. 5:28).

I caution and encourage young married couples on this issue: Please, please, carefully and deliberately discuss this issue together. Hopefully you will wrestle with this before the wedding, but if you haven't yet, come down from the clouds of wedded bliss long enough to talk about these tough financial issues. Do it before you get too far down the road and lose your way in the financial wilderness of poor planning and misplaced priorities.

If you set your mind to it, your family *can* make it on one income. Put God first and prioritize your future. God will take care of you—He's got your back. All He asks is that you humble yourself under His mighty hand and He will exalt you in due time. Cast all of your cares upon Him, because He cares for you (see 1 Pet. 5:6-7).

Out of Bondage, Into Freedom

God's will is not for us to be in financial bondage. The devil binds. God frees. His desire is for us to experience the fulfilling discipline of financial freedom!

It is Satan who has convinced us that the things of this world can meet our needs better than God can. This thinking leads to bondage. Financial freedom comes from God. If you have faith in God's Word and if you follow His process for dealing with money, He will provide for you.

Financial freedom requires discipline. If you're going to be financially free and successful, you've got to be disciplined. I'll tell you the truth:

It takes work! But it's worth it. Wouldn't you rather put forth a little effort to get out of bondage than stay in bondage for the rest of your life?

Many people today have allowed themselves to be swept into debt. Whether it's a closeout sale, an end-of-the-month deal, a low-interest credit card or a no-payment-for-30-days offer—they get swept right into debt because they don't exercise self-control and say no.

God has called us to discipline, to self-control, to the spirit of a sound mind. The fruit of the Spirit of God is love, joy, peace, longsuffering, kindness, goodness, faithfulness, gentleness and self-control (see Gal. 5:22-23) *in all areas*, including our financial affairs.

Are you of a sound mind in how you handle money? Only when you have this nailed down, only when you're able to practice self-control and discipline and the spirit of a sound mind, can you move from financial bondage into financial freedom.

Length of days is in [wisdom's] right hand, in her left hand riches and honor.

PROVERBS 3:16

Section III

Economics 101

Anyone who has ever tried giving up a bad habit knows that a key to long-term success is replacing that bad habit with a new *good* habit. The same holds true with finances.

In Section II, we examined various mistaken mind-sets that often exist in the Church with regard to money. Now we'll look at solid financial practices and strong frames of mind with which to replace those wrong mind-sets. To put it another way, now that we've seen what *not* to do, we're going to look at what *to* do.

A key part of this process is building your financial knowledge and understanding. This section will highlight key financial concepts, lay some economic groundwork, give you the spiritual theological insight necessary for optimal success, and equip you with a basic scriptural foundation for understanding the importance of achieving and maintaining financial health.

In this section, we will look at the three *T*s of money; foundational monetary basics; kingdom layaway; and the seven keys to making your money count.

Chapter 10

The Three *T*s of Money

The parable of the minas in Luke 19:11 reveals that money is a *tool*, a *test* and a *testimony*. Let's examine these three *T*s of money.

Money Is a *Tool*

We are responsible for properly utilizing the tools God gives us for the performance of our duties as His stewards. Read that sentence again. Money has been given to us as a *tool* for furthering His kingdom. It is not a possession! Thinking that money is yours to possess will lead you to fail worse than the third servant in the parable of the minas. Money is simply a tool, a medium of exchange in Earth's realm. It is the means by which wealth is transferred from the kingdom of darkness into the Kingdom of light.

Money should not be idolized or loved. It has no power sitting there by itself. There is no authority in it. It is amoral. It is inanimate. It's not even "the root of all evil," as so many people incorrectly state. The Bible says that *the love* of money is *a* root of all kinds of evil (see 1 Tim. 6:10).

In Luke 19, the nobleman's instructions were to take the mina—the *tool*—and do business with it. It's the same as if he would have left them with a trowel and told them to rejuvenate the garden with it—to dig out the weeds, turn the soil, create new crops—or if he would have told them to take a hammer and saw and create a new house. The money the master gave them was a tool: Take this tool and put it to work creating new assets!

The problem with the third servant was that he did not recognize that the money was a tool. He said in Luke 19:20, "I have kept . . ." He *kept* the master's money! He thought the money was a *possession*. He did not understand the dynamic of money as a tool with which to do business. Even though he received instructions to the contrary, he assumed that his master would be satisfied if he merely held on to it, buried it and hid it. No!—the master wanted him to increase it. Invest it. Do business with it.

Money is a tool by which God blesses and empowers His people. It is a tool by which He measures our commitment and spiritual relationship with Him and how trustworthy we are. When we begin to see that, then we're on our way to the next step . . .

Money Is a *Test*

The money given by the nobleman was also a *test*. The nobleman came back to see what the servants had done while he was gone.

The greatest areas of spiritual testing in our lives is not how many demons we cast out, how many sick people we heal or even whether we speak in tongues—it's how we handle the basic practicalities of life. Our salvation contract doesn't have an exclusion clause from the problems of life. When God saves us, it's not as if it will never rain on us again, or we'll never be attacked by the enemy, or we'll never face any more hardship. The evidence of our faith is not that we learn to go *around* the tests of life. Rather, it is that we go *through* the tests and come out on the other side with a testimony that says, "Nobody but God could have accomplished this!"

Money is a test to:

- Gauge our growth
- Ascertain our ability to obey and to learn
- Establish our rewards (for how well we pass the test)

The money the master gave the servants in Luke 19 to do business with was a test to gauge their growth. How do we know that? Because the master said to the one who handled it rightly, "You started with one. You gained ten. Now I'll give you ten cities to rule over" (see Luke 19:16-17). *Progression*. It's a process. The other servant earned five. The master said to him, "You started with one. Now you have five. I'll give you five cities" (see Luke 19:18-19). This process signifies progression and growth.

The gifts God has given each of us are not for us, per se—they are to be used to enhance and expand His kingdom. There will never be any more significant test in our lives than how we handle the material blessings God gives us.

The master of the servants gave, planted into their lives and said, "I want to see a return on this when I get back." He was testing them. He gave them the money (the tool) and he went away. When he got back, he expected a return. He had left them to their own, and when he returned, he wanted to find progress, growth and profit. It was a test.

God works the same way. He has planted something into every life. The question is, what kind of return is He getting on what He planted with you? To use an accounting term, He expects a return on investment (ROI) from each of us. Just as the master called the servants to account when he returned, Christ too will call us to an accounting. What kind of ROI is He getting with you right now? He has invested much in you and expects that investment to be profitable. One of the reasons He has stuck with some of us in spite of us is because He's hoping His investment in us might pay off someday. God will help us pass the test as long as we don't stop trying. The devil would have taken many of us out long ago if God hadn't prevented him from snatching victory from us.

When we handle money well, we prove ourselves worthy of handling true riches—spiritual riches. Luke 16:11 says, "If you have not been faithful in the unrighteous mammon, who will commit to your trust the true riches?" "Unrighteous mammon" means *money*. This does not mean unrighteous in the sense of bad or evil; it simply means that there's no virtue in a piece of money itself. *Unrighteous* in this usage means that while it's not holy, it's not necessarily unholy either. It's neutral. There's nothing spiritual about money itself. If you have not been able to handle plain old money, who will commit into your care the true riches?

If you prove yourself to be irresponsible in the way you handle earthly riches, you will be deprived of *true* riches. The word "true" puts things into a whole different light. The verse tantalizingly indicates that there is something deeper and more important than earthly riches. In other words, something more valuable and significant than mere money itself. The way in which we handle earthly riches—money—is an indicator of how (and *if*) we will be allowed to handle these better riches.

Money Is a *Testimony*

How many Christian millionaires are there? Each year, *Forbes* magazine issues two annual lists: he top 100 billionaires and the top 100 millionaires, from around the world. Check out that list and see for yourself how many of them are professing, believing Christians. If we Christians are claiming that our Father is so rich in houses and land, then why aren't many of us on those lists? There should be a lot more. I think it's because we Christians aren't as faithful in handling money as well as we should be and God cannot trust us with much of it!

Here is Jesus' commentary on that theory:

> Whoever can be trusted with very little can also be trusted with much, and whoever is dishonest with very little will also be dishonest with much. So if you have not been trustworthy in handling worldly wealth, who will trust you with true riches? And if you have not been trustworthy with someone else's property, who will give you property of your own? (Luke 16:10-12, *NIV*).

Money itself testifies against us if we are not handling money properly. People who go around saying things like, "If only I had a million dollars," are generally the same people who are perpetually broke, because most people would do pretty much the same thing with a million dollars that they do with 20 dollars.

Most people handle their new pay raise the same way they handled their last one: They spend it. They increase their "lifestyle." They keep up even more with the Joneses. They celebrate. They don't learn. They don't grow. The testimony of their money management prowess is that they're not learning a thing about God's process for money management. It's the rare person who possesses the wisdom to actually *invest* their raise *and* keep their lifestyle at the same level, thereby increasing their asset margin.

Why should there not be more Christians on the *Forbes* annual lists? For a Christian to handle money well is a living testimony to the rest of the world: When we handle money with astuteness, it speaks highly of our own Father and of our individual state of spiritual affairs. We must be faithful to compile a solid testimony concerning how we approach dealing with finances, because we *will* be held accountable for it when our Lord returns—and He told us we will be called to account when He comes back. The day will come when we each will hear God say, "You're next—it's *your* turn to appear before the judgment seat of Christ" (see 2 Cor. 5:10). On your day before Christ, He'll ask you to give an accounting—He told us that would happen, too, when He said, "And there is no creature hidden from His sight, but all things are naked and open to the eyes of Him to whom we must give account" (Heb. 4:13).

What kind of testimony are you building concerning the resources He has entrusted you with? What excuse will you come up with when He asks you what happened to the mina He left in your care? Is it buried in the ground? Did you spend it? Or is the mina He gave you earning even more minas?

Sometimes our testimony springs from simply clinging to God through the most difficult circumstances, including financial hardships. There are people who have a testimony not because they've been so good or so faithful or so kind, but because God led them up the mountain—and every time the devil tried to put an obstacle in their way, they followed God and He either led them around it or over it or through it. That's what a testimony is: When the enemy attacks, you trust God and hold on through it all. When the enemy attacks your finances, you trust God to pay your bills with a zero balance checking account and stay the course with due diligence. When the enemy puts questions in your mind, God gives you the power to resist the wiles of the devil.

A Living Example

In 3 John 2, the author writes, "Beloved, I pray that you may prosper in all things and be in health, just as your soul prospers."

God wants you to be a living example of *His* prosperity—a prosperity that includes both spiritual abundance and financial blessings. He wants you to be prosperous *in spite* of what's not in your pocket. *In spite* of what kind of car you drive. *In spite* of what kind of home you live in. *In spite* of what kind of clothes you wear. He wants you to have a prosperity anchored in the reality that money is only a tool, a test and a testimony for the true riches that lie beyond the material confines of this decaying world.

A favorite hymn of many Christians is a little song called "Amazing Grace." One of my favorite lines says:

Through many dangers, toils and snares
we have already come.
'Twas Grace that brought us safe thus far
and Grace will lead us home!

Don't be ashamed to testify that you have come through many "dangers, toils and snares." Don't be ashamed to share that the devil was trying to stop you every step of the way, yet God gave you the power and grace to climb the mountain and stand up like a champion to give Him all the praise. *God's grace* brought you through the snares so that you could be a living testimony of Him. Tried, tested and true—a honed tool in His hands, ready to serve Him to the utmost.

God says, "I will make your way prosperous." Your way is a journey. It's a trip, the process of arriving at your destination, of moving from one place to another. God says He will make you prosperous *along the way* of your journey. That's why you can have the mind-set of prosperity even before you've turned His one mina into 10.

God has given every Christian something on the inside that will hold us fast when the storms of life rage. He has put something inside of you that lets you shout for joy because He knows the plans He has for you—plans to *prosper* you (see Jer. 29:11).

Prosperity is God's favor on your life. It comes from learning to walk by faith and not by sight. It comes from learning to call those things that are *not* as though they already are. It's okay to walk like you've got a million dollars, even before you have that money in your pocket, because you already have prosperity inside of you: the Holy Spirit! There's something inside you that's bigger than everything on the outside.

God wants you to prosper in *everything*—which includes your finances. Do not allow the enemy to stop you. Do not allow people to stop you. Do not allow naysayers to stop you. Do not allow liars to stop you. Those people are not your source—God is your Source. And He is far more powerful than all the voices of the world combined. "Greater is he that is in you, than he that is in the world" (1 John 4:4, *KJV*).

God does not call His children to mediocrity! He calls us to *excellence*. God does not call His children to fail! He calls us to *succeed*. He calls us to stand on the mountaintop and declare that we got there by nothing but His grace alone! And since God desires that we prosper, settling for anything less would dishonor Him.

The covenant is not only about *us* getting blessed—it is about us *using God's blessings to bless those in need.* In his book *Prosperity with Purpose*, my friend Wendell Smith writes:

> True biblical prosperity has two purposes. First, God wants to bless His children and meet their needs . . . by helping us get jobs, pay our bills, invest our money wisely and save for the future. Secondly, the Lord wants to give us abundance so we can share it with others and help meet needs of those around us.[1]

It's about the assets we create, benefiting others. For example, as our church goes about being faithful in following God's process concerning our finances, our building, the Great Western Forum, creates a living testimony to God's Word and to His promises because it generates income and revenue that blesses others. When artists like Madonna and the Rolling Stones and Neil Diamond perform there, more than 500 people are working in our building. We are providing jobs. Our building creates income for those who work there. In short, our building turns a profit *for the benefit of others.*

The purpose of the profit is to penetrate the lives of the people of our community. We channel financial empowerment to the people who work there, and they become a channel to recycle their financial prosperity into the community in which they live. It is more than a plain ol' church building where people gather and pray and sing and shout. It is a building that encourages life, that promotes growth, that stands as a legacy to future generations of Christians, and that stands up as a testimony to God's process for taking care of business and making money count!

What is your testimony? Are you leaving a legacy for others? Are you using the money God has given you as a tool for blessing others and for expanding His kingdom? Are you passing God's test? Have you stopped living on the brink of debt and from paycheck to paycheck?

God has called us to be a living testimony in how we handle the money He gives us. If you're not passing His test, if you're not using His money to bless others, then it's time to change. If you're in a financial bind, if you've dug yourself into a hole, then get busy with rule number one: Start digging yourself out!

Robert Morris writes in *The Blessed Life*, "God wants to put great resources in our hands so we can be conduits of His blessing."[2] Those resources may be monetary and material like the rich young ruler who met Jesus, or they may be resources of mercy and compassion like Mother Teresa. Either way, financial bondage will hinder God's design for your life. Financial bondage will be the weak link in God's chain of blessing from you to the world. Make a commitment to God today to get yourself out of debt so that you can start contributing to God's kingdom and become a blessing to others.

Well done, good servant; because you were faithful in a very little, have authority over ten cities.

LUKE 19:17

Notes

1. Wendell Smith, *Prosperity with Purpose* (San Francisco: The City Church, 2005), p. 51.
2. Robert Morris, *The Blessed Life* (Ventura, CA: Regal Books, 2004), p. 145.

CHAPTER 11

Foundational Monetary Basics

There were also some who said,
"We have mortgaged our lands and vineyards and houses,
that we might buy grain because of the famine."
NEHEMIAH 5:3

To understand the basics of building wealth, we have to understand a few key concepts. They're not difficult to grasp, and they're very important to learn. First, let's take a look at some basic terminology . . .

Asset Versus Liability

One definition of "asset" is "sufficient property to pay debts." Assets pay off debts, thus freeing up money to make more money. Assets carry intrinsic monetary value. Assets do not generally depreciate in value in and of themselves—they create value. They *are* value.

On the other hand, a *liability*, according to *Webster's*, is "something for which one is liable; especially: pecuniary obligation: DEBT, a disadvantage."[1] Liabilities *take away* money or value. They are an expense, a cost. They represent a depletion of assets.

Benjamin Franklin once said, "In this world, nothing can be said to be certain, except death and taxes."[2] As this popular quote reminds us, we can always count on certain liabilities in life, and one of the biggest is taxes. The tax rate now is such that we work from January until approximately the middle of May before we start making any money for ourselves. The government gets their portion of our income before most people even see it. Taxes are our first expense—they hit us before our employer even cuts us a paycheck.

Another liability that has us working for it is the bank. The vast majority of people who supposedly "own" their home do not own it free and clear. They work, in effect, for the bank, because they owe money to that financial institution for their home loan. They may work at XYZ Corp from nine to five, but they really work *for* the mortgage lender.

Nehemiah 5:3 details a situation that had overtaken the people of Israel. They were actually mortgaging their homes and borrowing money in order to pay their taxes! Perhaps you know someone in a similar situation. That is not God's plan. He has called us to something far better.

Asset Creation

God wants us to build our assets, not our liabilities. To their detriment, many people do just the opposite. They continually increase their liabilities without ever thinking about how to grow their assets. If we want to increase our wealth, we must spend money on things that will create and build assets.

Don't focus so much on the money itself. Think instead about what you *do* with the money. How do you know whether something is an asset or a liability? If it will ultimately make money or increase monetary value, it is an asset. If not, it is a liability. Assets *make* money. Liabilities *take* money.

Make a decision to spend more on assets and less on liabilities. Try to take on as few liabilities as possible while always looking for ways to increase your assets.

Increasing Assets Through Investments

To *invest* means, "To commit money or capital in order to gain a financial return."[3] When you invest, you expect a return on your investment. Increasing one's assets requires that a person "do business" (or invest) for the purpose of making a profit. Investing, by definition, calls for multiplying. We are to *multiply* the money we're given through investment. We are to *turn a profit.*

Assets are not always in cash form. An asset can be any object of significant value. When you own a home, for instance, you build up *equity* in that house—money that you can redeem in the form of cash when you sell the house. Your home, therefore, is an asset once its value exceeds what you owe to the bank.

There are things that could be an asset for somebody else, but a liability for you. For example, if you can't afford a $300,000 home or if you can't pay it off in a reasonable amount of time, then getting a mortgage on that house could be a liability, because you'll owe money to the bank for decades. That's not to say you shouldn't purchase a home. If you're able to pay off a $200,000 home loan in a reasonable amount of time and it is in a location that has potential for increasing in value, then getting that mortgage would be wise.

If you want to be smart at building your assets, you need to keep tuned in to market trends and values. Do your homework. Research and up-to-date information is essential. Stay on top of market fluctuations. If it's real estate you're considering as an investment, buy a home in a neighborhood that your research shows is experiencing an upswing in value each year, not one that's declining. By the time you've paid off your mortgage, you should be able to sell the home for significantly more than what you bought it for.

Making intelligent, informed business decisions that will reap profits and not produce liabilities is what creating and increasing assets is all about.

Producer Versus Consumer

We must also learn the difference between being a consumer and being a producer. A *producer* is someone who gives form and shape to something. He creates, he brings into existence, he builds, he makes. A *consumer*, according to *Webster's*, is "one that consumes . . . one that utilizes economic goods."[4] Most people are consumers. We buy things. We buy a whole lot of "stuff." But few of us actually *produce* what is being purchased. To be successful financially, you must draw a clear distinction between the two—and then learn to produce more than you consume!

Stewardship

Money counts when we learn to oversee it as a trust of stewardship bestowed upon us by God, then respond to that trust by becoming channels and conduits through which others are blessed.

Stewardship is one of the most important concepts that we must understand and master if we hope to accomplish anything for God's kingdom. *Stewardship*, according to *Webster's*, is "the conducting, supervising, or managing of something; *especially*: the careful and responsible management of something entrusted to one's care."[5] Christian stewardship takes the definition a step further: Stewardship is how you handle whatever God gives over to your control or possession.

In the Luke 19 parable of the minas, each servant, each *steward*, started with the same amount, but the results were vastly different. At the heart of the differing results was how each servant understood and put the principle of stewardship into practice. One servant turned his one mina into 10. Another turned his one into five. And one did nothing with his mina except bury it in the ground—representing the worst possible stewardship of the nobleman's money other than outright stealing it.

Built into the principle of stewardship is the concept of *just reward*. Each servant was rewarded according to how well he managed his master's money. The servant who gained 10 minas received authority over 10 cities. The servant who gained five minas received authority over five cities. But the man who did nothing at all with his mina received nothing at all.

The parable suggests that *all* of us are stewards of what the King—God—owns. If we hope to receive a good reward, we need to practice good stewardship and invest wisely what the King has given us—not bury it like the third servant did. Many Christians get into trouble because they forget this important point. They make the mistake of thinking that the money God entrusts into their care is their own personal property to do with as they please. But as the Bible makes very clear in the parable of the minas, the money belonged to the nobleman and the servants were given control of it for a short season only. It all belonged to the nobleman in the first place.

To be good stewards, we must transfer ownership of everything we own—or rather, everything we *think* we own—back to God. Surrender all rights of ownership to Him. That means not only what you *possess*, but also what you *owe*. Surrender to Him your bills and your debts, as well. Some people might think, "You know, I've made such a mess. I'd be embarrassed giving this chaos to God." But you have no choice. When it gets that bad, who else can you give it to who can fix it?

I guarantee you, once you give it over to God, then it's not your problem anymore. Listen to Him as He tells you how to take care of those bills, because it's His problem now. He'll tell you how to take care of that debt. He'll give you the provision to pay it all off and He'll tell you when to do so. Tune in to Him and He will guide you as you submit yourself to Him as a steward.

Being a steward doesn't mean being a beggarly slave. Joseph was a steward, and he rose to the position of running the entire household of Potiphar, captain of Pharaoh's elite palace guard. Then he rose to become second-in-command only to Pharaoh himself. He was even trusted enough to oversee operation of the jail when he was a prisoner there! Now *that* is the heart of a steward! Joseph prospered with every blessing that comes along with being a good steward.

Just as there's reward for good stewardship, there's also punishment for poor stewardship: having it taken away from us. In the parable of the minas, the third man didn't just miss out on a reward like the other two servants—he actually *lost* the money that had been entrusted to his care in the first place. Since he proved that he didn't know how to handle money, the master announced that the little bit he did have was to be taken from him. And the master didn't just take it and give it to somebody who didn't have any. He didn't take it from the third man and give it to the poor or poverty-stricken. The Bible says the master took it from the third servant and gave it to the man who had *the most* (see Luke 19:24). Why? Because that man had shown himself to be the most astute in handling the nobleman's assets. He proved himself the most trustworthy and efficient steward of them all in monetary matters.

We are each responsible for what we are given, to handle it in a manner that honors and exemplifies the King. It is urgent that we Christians learn this biblical principle. God is calling us into a season of revelation and understanding of a fundamental biblical principle that few have learned or understood before. It is a spiritual principle that works even in the pragmatic constructs of the world—but that is no reason why the world should understand and exercise it in many cases better than we Christians do!

Notes

1. *Merriam-Webster's Online Dictionary*, s.v. "liability." http://www.m-w.com/dictionary/liability (accessed March 2007).
2. Benjamin Franklin (1706–1790), letter to Jean-Baptiste Leroy, November 13, 1789.
3. *The American Heritage® Dictionary of the English Language*, fourth edition, s.v. "invest," Dictionary.com. http://dictionary.reference.com/browse/invest (accessed March 2007).
4. *Merriam-Webster's Online Dictionary*, s.v. "consumer."
5. Ibid., s.v. "stewardship."

CHAPTER 12

Kingdom Layaway

The wealth of the sinner is stored up for the righteous.

PROVERBS 13:22

Have you ever used a department store layaway plan, maybe for a couch, dining room furniture, refrigerator or clothes? There aren't many stores that offer layaway plans anymore. Where I grew up in East St. Louis, almost every store on the main drag, Collinsville Avenue, had layaway. Layaway was a common type of purchase agreement in those days. The way it works is that you pay a small deposit on the item and request that the store hold it for you on layaway—they keep it while you make payments on the balance due. Once you pay them in full, they release the item to you. God also has a layaway plan—one that benefits us, His children.

Redeeming the Layaway

When I was growing up, we used to buy a lot of things on layaway. A few dollars down, a few dollars a week. We would choose something on the rack, and because we said we were going to buy it, they took it off the rack and put it on reserve while we made payments. It was held in the stockroom until we stepped up and took it, paid in full. (A couple times we left something on layaway so long we forgot it was there!)

Likewise, God says that the wealth currently being held on reserve in the stockroom under the control of the unrighteous is actually on layaway for the righteous and the just. This is what Proverbs 13:22 means when it says, "the wealth of the sinner is stored up for the righteous." The term "laid up" means "to be covered for protection." The Hebrew root for "laid up" is *tsaphan*, which means, "to hide, treasure or store up." In other words, wealth that is under the control of the sinner—the world system—is covered, protected and kept *on reserve* for the righteous until it's time for us to redeem it. The world does not realize it, but their wealth is on layaway for God's children.

The question is, how do we get the wealth of the sinner? How do we redeem it and transfer it to the Kingdom of heaven? First, we have to understand that the world system works under a different principle than the Kingdom's system. The world system works under the process of buying and selling, while God's system works under the principle of giving and receiving. We have to operate within the world's rules if we want to transfer their wealth to God's kingdom—nobody is going to just give the world's wealth over to us! We can't just go out and name it, claim it and frame it in the name of Jesus and take it on home. That's a good shout, but it won't get you your blessing. In order to get the wealth transferred to us, we have to operate within the world's system of buying and selling with money. Once we receive the wealth of the sinner, we can apply to it God's system of giving and receiving.

When Deuteronomy 8:18 says that God gives us the "power" to gain wealth, it means He gives us the ability and resources (money or the means to get money) that enable us to prevail in a system controlled by the world. When we take control of any portion of the world's wealth ("the wealth of the sinner," as Proverbs 13:22 refers to it), we are taking control of land, houses, tangible items, businesses, assets and so on that we did not create but that were "on hold" for us until we received them.

For example, when you as a believer purchase a house or a piece of property that existed before you bought it, God gave you the power, the resources, the ability, to make that transaction within the world's system of buying and selling. Every time you accumulate such assets, you are transferring them from the kingdom of darkness and bringing them into God's kingdom. At this point, God really starts watching you closely, to see what you do with that wealth you just appropriated from the world.

He watches us closely at this point because when we believers apply God's principals and processes to the world's system, the "wealth" we gain is given into our control with the proviso that once we retrieve such wealth from the world, we then *transfer it to the benefit of the Kingdom of light and to the glory of God*. We are not to hoard it for ourselves—to lay it away in the back room never to be redeemed. We are not to let it sit gathering moths, dust and rust. It is given to us for the *benefit of God's kingdom and others*. We are blessed to bless others.

Look at it this way: If you, as a husband and father who brings home an income, don't use your income for the benefit of your family and instead keep it for your own selfish wants, of what benefit is that income to your family? None! Your family suffers. I can't tell you how many families I know that have suffered because money given by God is used for the abuse of alcohol, drugs or pornography. That money is not yours to do with as you please! The income you are blessed to earn is meant to benefit your family and the family of God.

Kingdom Layaway Redeemed

The church I pastor is in a building that we did not build, but God decreed that the building, which had been on holy layaway for His children, was to be released to the kingdom of God at His appointed time. When we bought the building, we didn't just buy a big sports arena; we transferred into the Kingdom system something that was built by the world system. We took something that was actually built for *us* to occupy at a time foreordained by God. And now it is sanctified, made holy, consecrated by the presence of the living God who owns it. The wealth that was in the hands of sinners was on layaway for the righteous who now own and operate the building.

During the times when Faithful Central Bible Church is not holding services, the building is used for concerts, for sporting events such as basketball, wrestling and ice shows, and for other public events. The world still comes in and uses our building, but they now pay the church to rent it. And they pay us well! Every time they pay us, more wealth that would have been recycled through the world system is transferred to the kingdom of God. This, my friend, is the real deal on "the end-time transfer of wealth" that we hear about so often!

How about you? Are you redeeming those things that God has on layaway for you? There are treasures currently stored up for you, treasures that are in the hands of sinners that belong to you as God's righteous child. Are you in the process of redeeming those treasures? If not, what's stopping you?

Ephesians 1:3 says, "Blessed be the God and Father of our Lord Jesus Christ, who has blessed us with every spiritual blessing in the Heavenly places in Christ." The past tense of the verb "blessed" indicates that God *has already* blessed us with the spiritual blessings in the heavenly places—they're on heavenly layaway for us. Thus, we have the earthly ability, we have the spiritual blessing and we have God leading us—what more do we need?

Personally, I don't want to get to heaven and come across a ledger that lists all the things God had on reserve for me that I failed to take possession of because I was inattentive, incompetent or, worse, disobedient! Remember, it is the righteous, the obedient, those who follow God's ways, who are rewarded with prosperity: "Misfortune pursues the sinner, but prosperity is the reward of the righteous" (Prov. 13:21, *NIV*).

Chapter 13

Seven Keys to Making Your Money Count

Pay attention to my wisdom; lend your ear to my understanding.

Proverbs 5:1

To succeed at something as pragmatic as finances, it helps to follow practical guidelines and to heed the financial wisdom and understanding of others. Whether you're in debt and looking for ways to dig yourself out or are simply looking for ways to increase your sustainability, here are seven ways you can make the most of your finances.

Key 1:
Spend Less than You Make

To one degree or another, all of us have an understanding of our basic monthly monetary outgo, yet many find themselves surprised by how little they have left over at the end of the month. If you're constantly wrestling with having less than you thought, the solution is simple: Learn to spend less than you make!

Once you've paid your basic expenses, how much money do you have left? Remember, the financial resources you receive are to be used as a tool. They are given to you by God as a tool to do business with. But if you're burning up the tool each month, how are you going to build any wealth?

The Church is doing a great disservice in this area. Church leaders go to conferences and shout, "Everybody be prosperous!" but they don't teach people that a foundation of basic economics must be laid first. That foundation is this: The 2 you earned, added to the 2 in your bank account, equals 4—and if you're spending 5, you've lost it all *and* you're in debt! If you keep bringing in 4 and spending 5, I promise you that God will not let you have 8 or 16 or 32—not until you learn to handle 4 properly, His way.

Key 2:
Cut Up Those Cards!

Proverbs 22:7 states, "The rich rules over the poor, and the borrower is servant to the lender." The statement "the borrower is servant to the lender" is one that our culture flatly rejects, but it is completely true: If we go around borrowing money here, there and everywhere, we replace God as our need-meeter and serve our lenders instead of Him. We replace Him with credit, loans and credit cards. Sadly, this is what is happening to many people today—credit has become their god.

You want to send up an offering to the Lord? Make an offering of those credit cards! Put them on the altar and set a match to them! Burn 'em up! There's a time and a place for credit cards, but many people are not disciplined enough to use them as they should be used. Get with some friends who are also in bondage to credit cards and have a burnt-offering party! Set them ablaze and dance around the flames as the smoke rises to the Lord as a sacrifice of selfishness, greed and materialism.

Until you gain the self-control to spend less than you make, get rid of the charge cards. Those things are sending you to credit card hell. Eradicating them will eliminate the temptation to buy junk you can live without and will help set you on the path to putting your money to work for you. If you can't pay them off every month (which is really using them as cash), they will take you down, my friend! I can promise you that. And trying to pay off the balance by paying the minimum monthly payment is almost a mathematical impossibility. Been there, done that! (At least, I tried!) Trust me, it will kill you financially. It is a sinkhole you cannot swim out of without God's help.

Key 3:
Talk to Your Creditors

It is not God's will for you to be in debt and enslaved to creditors. We live in a culture that tells people that "we are what we own," so it's easy to fall prey to the mentality that we must spend, spend, spend and buy on credit in order to live as large as society tells us we should. The result is an alarming number of people up to their eyeballs in debt because of material possessions–house, car, boat, goodies, toys, off-road vehicles, ski-doos, a second house, a vacation place, clothes in the closet with price tags still on them–all in the name of keeping up with the Joneses.

If you find yourself in debt and struggling to keep up with your payments, one of the first things you need to do is contact the person or organization you owe money to, whether it's the bank, the credit card company or the department store. The best way to do that is in person. If the creditor is nearby, go to their office. If that isn't feasible because they're too far away, write them a letter.

Whether by letter or in person, always be very courteous and professional. If you meet them personally, don't show up licking an ice cream cone wearing shoes that blink in the dark, a fluorescent tie and an oily jacket that has a motorcycle embroidered across the back. Look professional. Dress conservatively. Remember, you're on their turf and you owe them money. They need assurance that you are a solid person who they can trust.

The next-best thing to a personal appearance is a well-written letter (not an e-mail–an actual letter). The letter should be neatly typed and easy to read. Don't scrawl it on a brown paper bag. Don't write it in pencil. Don't use your daughter's crayons. Definitely don't write in chicken-scratch handwriting. It must be typed up and printed out.

Whether you meet in person or write a letter, the message will be the same. Introduce yourself and explain why you haven't been making your payments. Apologize and explain that you have been unable to keep up with your payments because of extenuating circumstances. Show them that you are concerned about this and that you want to make it right. Always tell the truth. Be honest with them about why you haven't been paying. Don't lie. Don't fudge it. Don't come up with some lame excuse to try to justify your irresponsibility. You blew it, you're sorry, you'll fix it. Explain that you expect your circumstances to improve, whether that's because of a new job, going back to school, a new budgeting system, whatever. Then give them a timeframe for when you expect to be able to pay off your debt. Be humble! Cut a deal!

A word of warning: Don't make promises you can't keep. Set up a system you can actually abide by. Don't promise to pay them back by next month just to satisfy them, when you know full well that the earliest you can pay them back is next year. Ecclesiastes says that it's "better not to vow than to vow and not pay" (Eccles. 5:5). If you vow to do something, do it. If you tell someone you're going to make the payments, make them. Most creditors will be very open to setting up some sort of terms or payment plan once they realize how serious you are about paying them back.

Occasionally debt can be too big, too heavy, too overwhelming and your creditors don't even want to talk to you. In those extreme cases, you might need outside guidance. If so, go to a fellow Christian who is a professional in these matters. The Bible says, "Blessed is the man who walks not in the counsel of the ungodly" (Ps. 1:1). You would no more look for water from a rock than you would seek godly advice from a non-Christian!

If you find yourself in need of professional help, seek out a reputable Christian counseling agency that gives solid advice that matches up with God's Word. They should be able to assess your situation and construct a plan that's tailor-made to fit your needs and get you out of debt. Contact your local Better Business Bureau and request information on the company to make sure they're a legitimate firm with a good reputation and a solid track record. If they can't handle their own business, you can't expect them to help you handle yours.

Key 4:
Itemize Your Expenses

For one month, keep track of everything that you and your family pay for, both goods and services. Include even minor items such as toll road fees, cups of coffee, chewing gum, parking fees, *everything*. At the end of the month, you might be surprised at how much you're spending!

Go through that list and identify areas where you can either eliminate expenses or opt for less expensive alternatives, such as buying generic brands, shopping at 99-cent stores and discount department stores, or renting a DVD for a family night at home instead of taking the entire family out to a movie.

Sometimes making simple changes to your schedule can also save you a lot of money. For instance, if you buy your lunch every day, try getting up a few minutes early in the morning to pack a lunch instead. This could save you $20 a week or more, which could add up to over a $1,000 per year in savings. Get creative! Get the whole family involved. Have fun with it!

Key 5:
Reduce Your Debt

In Matthew 5:14-16, Jesus says, "You are the light of the world . . . Let your light so shine before men, that they may see your good works and glorify your Father in Heaven." Christians are to be an example and a light in all that we do, and this applies to how we handle our debts and bills. How do we do that?

First, sit down and itemize all of your debt. This includes credit card debt, mortgage, car payment, school loans, overdue bills, and so forth. Calculate the exact up-to-date amount for each.

Once you have a list of all your creditors, start paying each one off, one at a time. If you're struggling to pay your regular monthly bills, pay off the small ones first. Same with past-due debt: If you have a $25 monthly light bill and a $110 monthly phone bill, pay off the light bill, *then* the phone bill. Pay off the $500 credit card, and *then* the $1,200 medical bill. There are two reasons for this:

1. Paying something off entirely gives you a psychological boost from the accomplishment of seeing a debt or bill eliminated.

2. Sometimes it's just too difficult to tackle the big ones first.

When it comes to paying off debts that carry interest charges (such as credit cards, home loans, school loans, car loans), start by paying the debt with the *highest interest rate* first and then move down the list. In the long run, this will save you a lot of money that you would otherwise be paying to the bank or credit card company in interest. Depending on how much debt you have, this could save you hundreds, even thousands, of dollars each year in interest and fees that you'll no longer have to pay.

As you continue to pay off your debt, it is crucial that you maintain your current standard of living—don't start living large because you paid off your car loan and no longer have to send $320 to the credit union each month. Don't think you can go out and spend that money on a new wardrobe you don't really need or on a second flat-screen TV or on your third DVD player. Live within your means and put that $320 toward paying off other debt. When you reach the point where you have no more debt (that *will* happen eventually!), *invest* most or all of those payments you're saving. Financial freedom is the goal!

Key 6:
Invest, Invest, Invest!

Once you have learned to manage your monthly income so that you are taking in more than you're paying out, it's time to put the surplus to work. Like the faithful servants in Luke 19, *invest*! Do your homework and build an investment portfolio that meets your needs and your financial capabilities. Remember, higher returns come from higher risk, but high-risk investments might not be best for you. Most people opt for a diversified portfolio with steady returns—not too high of a risk, but more of a return than a simple savings account.

If you're not investment savvy yourself, seek out a reputable investment firm or qualified professional who can give you solid advice. Make sure you're dealing with a Christian person in a legitimate firm, with a solid reputation and proven past results. Do your homework. If they don't give good investment advice to their other clients, chances are they won't do you much good, either. The same applies to real estate investing: Seek out a reputable, licensed Christian agent to guide and assist you.

The key is to invest. Period. Don't hide your money in a hanky like the third servant. Put your money to work for God by investing it!

Key 7:
At the Very Least, Save!

How do you handle the material blessings that God has given you? You don't want to hear what the slothful servant heard the master say to him in Luke 19:23: "You could have at least put my money in the bank so that I might have collected interest." Simply saving your money is not as good as investing, but if you're not going to do anything else, at the very least put your money into a savings or money market account and earn a little bit of interest.

Shop around to find the best interest rate available. You'll be in for the long haul if you decide to gain wealth by relying on today's savings account interest rates to grow your money, but it's better than stashing it under a mattress.

Seven Ways to Get Extra Money

When it comes to finding money for paying off your debts, here's where you get to be creative. There are tons of ways to create money for paying off debts—any single one of them will be beneficial by itself, but the sum of them all will be incredible. Some of these will be fun. Some will be tough. Some will be short-term pain for long-term gain. If you put all of the following ideas to work, you'll be amazed at how quickly your debts get paid off.

The following list is by no means all-inclusive—get creative and brainstorm other methods for earning and saving money that can go toward the goal. The more you do, the quicker your debt will be eliminated.

1. Use Unexpected Gifts

Whenever you get unexpected money, use it to pay off debt. This includes birthday checks, Christmas gifts and anniversary money. Decide in advance that you will not spend it on yourself! Another source of money you can use to pay off your debt is your income tax refund. That's money you don't have yet, so you're not living on it. It's a windfall. Take it and apply it toward your debts.

2. Tap Your Savings Account

Another source for paying off your debts is the money in your savings account. It's better for you to be debt-free and have little or no savings than to have heavy debts and extra money in the bank. (This does not include your three- to six-month emergency savings fund.) I know what you're thinking: "What if I need that money?" You can come up with all the different hypothetical situations you want, but the Bible always stays the same:

> God shall supply *all* your need according to His riches in glory by Christ Jesus (Phil. 4:19, emphasis added).

Once you've paid off your debts, start putting your additional earnings back into your savings account. Before you know it, you'll have no debt, you'll have a solid savings account and you can begin investing.

3. Save Extra Money

Saving money has to be a family affair. Get the whole family involved. Hold a family meeting where you brainstorm creative ways to cut down on expenses. Come equipped with all your bills in hand, and work together to figure out which bills can be cut down or eliminated. Some ideas include:

1. *Set monthly phone time limits for each family member.* Once you hit your limit, hang up—you're done!

2. *Cancel one of your phones.* Do you really need more than two or three cell phones? Maybe you can cancel your landline and just use your cell phone(s). Figure out what works best for you and your family, with *saving money* as your guiding principle.

3. *Cancel the cable.* For some people this might be like giving up food, but it doesn't have to be that painful! Instead of watching cable TV shows, go to the local library and borrow

movies to watch at home together—they're free! You might find yourself spending more time together as a family, too!

4. *Save energy*. Energy bills can be expensive. If you live in a cold region, make the most of your energy by putting plastic over your windows during the wintertime and using space heaters. If you're in warmer regions, do you really need to have the air-conditioner so cold that you have to wear a sweater inside? Adjusting the thermostat even a few degrees can save a lot of money.

5. *Reduce grocery expenses*. Buying off-brand items can amount to incredible savings. You might be surprised how much the generic brands taste like the "real thing." That's because many national brand companies sell their products to generic labelers and grocery chains!

6. *Budget for clothing*. Do your kids *really* need $125 tennis shoes every few months? There's another area where you can buy off-brand and save a lot of money. If your kids are adamant about having the name-brand, let them know they'll need to earn the extra money themselves to pay the difference. (But if they're young and still growing quickly, forget the name brands!)

7. *Sell that second car*. Does your family have more than one car but can actually get by on only one? Sell the extra car for cash and put the money toward paying off your debts. You'll save money in gas, wear-and-tear, maintenance and insurance. If you *really* need a second car, double up with other family members as much as possible and share rides in order to save on gas and wear-and-tear.

As you can see, there are *many* ways your family can work together to reduce expenses and save money, money that can then be applied toward paying off your debt. Work together to find ways that work for you.

4. Work More to Earn More

The fourth way to get extra money to pay off your debt more quickly is to earn more money. If you have a job, work overtime. If you have only a part-time job, get a second one. Remember, it's not a permanent lifestyle change—it's just until those debts get eliminated.

If you can't land a part-time job somewhere, get creative and put your skills to work. If you're handy with tools, offer to repair things for co-workers or neighbors. If you're good with arts and crafts, go to a weekend arts and craft fair and get ideas there for things you might be able to make that you can sell.

The only caution in getting a part-time job or working overtime is to make sure that you don't deprive your family. If you're married with or without kids, be careful not to encroach on important personal time with your family. Don't break one biblical principle in order to keep another! Family is more important than money, so make sure you're spending time with them—though that doesn't mean you should go overboard with your family and take time away from your normal work schedule to be with them. It's all about balance, about being responsible. Don't work so much overtime that your family suffers, but keep in mind that it's a temporary situation you have to go through until your debt is wiped out.

Another issue is whether or not your wife should work (which we discussed in chapter 9). A rule of thumb on this is *children*. If there are still children in the home, God's pattern is that the wife be at home with them. If the wife is already working, you need to determine how much longer she has to work in order for you to get out of debt. Set that time-frame goal and stick to it. Titus contains some wisdom on this topic:

> Admonish the young women to love their husbands, to love their children, to be discreet, chaste, homemakers, good, obedient to their own husbands, that the word of God may not be blasphemed (Titus 2:4-5).

5. Buy in Bulk

Buying off-brands isn't the only way to save money at the store. In addition to buying generic, join together with two or three other families and buy your food in bulk. Split the cost and divide the food among you. Bulk foods are typically priced much more economically than standard-sized products, so buy in bulk and watch the savings add up! There are many bulk food stores (such as Costco and Sam's Club) that offer huge savings.

6. Eat at Home

One of the most often overlooked ways to save money is to eat at home. Restaurants are very expensive. This applies to all your meals, including lunch. If you're a businessman, did you know you can easily spend $150 to $200 a week just by eating at restaurants each day? Even though your company might pick up some of the tab, it still gets very expensive. Instead, swallow your pride, pack a lunch and eat at work!

When it comes to eating dinners at home, make it fun by getting together with other families. Take turns eating at each other's houses. You can end up saving quite a bit of money by spreading the cost around. It also builds fellowship as you spend time together on a regular basis.

7. Hold a Garage Sale

Garage sales are good ways to get rid of things that have been accumulating in your attic or garage and turn them into cash. Use the cash to put toward your bills and pay off your debts. Make a list of all the items you're considering selling, and then use the following guidelines to determine if you should hold on to it or sell it:

1. *Will keeping this item increase your effectiveness for the kingdom of God?* Your ultimate aim in life is to serve God and further His kingdom. How well does this item help you to do that? Does it actually hinder you? If it *does* increase your effectiveness, mark "yes" next to the item. If it *doesn't*, mark "no."

2. *Is this item absolutely essential?* In other words, is this item something that you absolutely need, or do you just want it? If it is genuinely essential, mark "yes" next to the item. If it is *not*, mark "no."

3. *Does this item contribute directly to your family unity and harmony?* This is a touchy subject because there might be things that are going to cause a bit of family discussion on whether or not to get rid of it. If it *does* contribute to family unity, mark "yes." If it *doesn't* contribute to family unity and/or it promotes disunity, mark "no."

4. *Is this item the most economical option?* For example, if you have two new cars, can you reduce that down to one by selling them both and buying a solid used car? The same thing applies to computers: Does every family member need his or her own computer, or can the family get by fine with just one or two? If the item *is* the most affordable option, mark "yes." If it *is not*, mark "no."

5. *Does this item provide more time for your family?* For example, if you have a big flat-screen TV, does it promote family time—

or does it take the husband away from the family on Saturdays and Sundays when all the ball games are on? If the item *promotes* quality family time, mark "yes." If it *does not* promote quality family time, mark "no."

6. *Is the value of the item increasing or going down?* Some things go up in value over time, but most things decrease. If it *is* increasing in value, mark "yes." For all other items, mark "no."

After you've answered all these questions for an item, add up the number of yeses and the number of nos to determine if you should hold on to an item or sell it. If you have more yeses, keep it. If you have more nos, sell it. Do this for each item you might potentially sell in a garage sale.

Answer these questions for items you're still paying off, too—whether it's a television, barbecue grill, car, whatever. If you have a family, turn this decision-making process into a family project—get everyone involved so that all will feel they're contributing to eliminating the family debt.

These easy steps will go a long way toward turning your finances around, but they're actually just the tip of the iceberg. After you have mastered these steps, continue to educate yourself on financial matters and how to put your money to work for you so that you can wisely handle the money God has given you.

The world's system is devised—at best—to teach us how to earn money by working at a job. At worst, it only teaches us how to spend, spend, spend and how to throw money away on things we really can live just fine without, things that don't enhance our lives. Many shortsighted, untrained people even give up important, long-lasting things in exchange for purchasing things that are temporary, unproductive and unnecessary. That is not God's way. God desires that we use money with discretion and wisdom so that we can invest in the expansion of His kingdom.

God's Wisdom Concerning Money

There is no area that will test your relationship with God more than your relationship with money. How you handle money is a testament to how you relate to God. As God's children, we are called—in fact, *commanded*—to pay attention to His wisdom concerning money.

Wisdom is so primary with God that Proverbs says it was the very first thing He brought forth before He set about creating the world: "The LORD brought me [wisdom] forth as the first of his works, before his deeds of old; I was appointed from eternity, from the beginning, before the world began" (Prov. 8:22-23, *NIV*).

This may come as a shock to some readers, but diligently seeking wisdom actually brings us *money, riches* and *prosperity*! Take a look at what the Bible has to say about the connection between wisdom and money:

> Length of days is in her [wisdom's] right hand,
> In her left hand riches and honor (Prov. 3:16).

> With me [wisdom] are riches and honor,
> enduring wealth and prosperity (Prov. 8:18, *NIV*).

> [Wisdom is] bestowing wealth on those who love me
> and making their treasuries full (Prov. 8:21, *NIV*).

Are you ready and willing to follow God's monetary wisdom? Are you prepared to adhere to His ways? To follow practical steps in your life that will grow your finances? Don't be set in old ways. Don't become complacent with the status quo. *Grow!* Wisdom should tell you that if you aren't busy taking new financial turf for the growth of God's kingdom, then you're losing your own financial turf to the enemy.

Qui non proficit, deficit!

Latin saying, meaning, "Who does not advance, recedes!"

SECTION IV

Moving Forward

Now that we've examined the dos and don'ts of finances and have reviewed some basic financial terminology and tips for success, let's move forward and examine God's plan for financial success.

How we handle money is important, but there is more to the lessons here than just our ability to handle money wisely. As we grow in our financial capabilities, it's important to grow spiritually as well, to send our roots deeper into God's truth.

Making your money count for God is a process whereby once you've mastered one area, you move up to the next. Never be complacent with where you are. The person who stops learning stops growing. If you want to be successful, you must continue to build on your knowledge and understanding so that God can bless you with increasing riches—which includes more than just monetary wealth, as Luke 16:11 indicates:

> If you have not been faithful in the unrighteous mammon, who will commit to your trust the true riches?

Jesus spoke the words of Luke 16:11 right after telling the parable of the unjust steward. In this parable, the steward is about to have his stewardship taken away from him because it's rumored that he is mismanaging his master's money. His master says, "Give an account of your stewardship, for you can no longer be steward" (Luke 16:2). In a last-ditch effort to ingratiate himself to his master's debtors, the steward sets about to "fix" the books and reduce the amounts they owe his master, so that after he loses his job they'll give him financial assistance because they benefited from his scheme:

> I have resolved what to do, that when I am put out of the stewardship, they may receive me into their houses. So he called every one of his master's debtors to him, and said to the first, "How much do you owe my master?" And he said, "A hundred measures of oil." So he said to him, "Take your bill, and sit down quickly and write fifty" (Luke 16:4-6).

This unjust steward instructs the debtors to write down a report that is not true—and the master *commends* him for it! Though the steward had dealt shrewdly with the master's money by manipulating the financial records (and there is even an insinuation that what he had done was fraudulent), the master clearly thinks it was clever and laudable:

> So the master commended the unjust steward because he had dealt shrewdly (Luke 16:8).

The steward's motive was right. *His method was wrong.* There are people who interpret this parable to mean that the steward was being praised for his deceptiveness. However, the praise he received had nothing to do with his being fraudulent or deceitful, but for being clever and for *understanding how money operates in the world.*

Jesus closed the parable with a dismal comparison between God's people and nonbelievers, indicting the former—*us*—for falling short on monetary matters:

> For the sons of this world are more shrewd in their generation than the sons of light (Luke 16:8).

When Jesus said that the sons of the world are more shrewd in their generation than the sons of light, He was saying that the world understands money principles, the dynamics of asset management and how to handle material blessings (money, business and finances) better than the Church does.

There are principles of handling money that God has implanted into the "cosmos," so to speak, that work for *anybody* who applies them. This text implies that the world has learned to utilize these principles better than we Christians have. If we aren't learning God's principles of handling financial blessings, that failure is a reflection on our relationship with Him. We are claiming that our Father is rich in houses and land, yet we can't even pay our basic expenses—and generally not because we don't have the money, but because we've been irresponsible when we do have it.

It is a shameful comment on Christianity that the world has learned to handle financial matters better than the Church has—especially since it *all* belongs to God in the first place. As Christians, we should reflect our Father in how we handle monetary affairs. We need to be not merely worldly-wise but *better* than the world at being wise. We need to be known as *the experts* when it comes to money matters. We should be the ones the world comes to when they need financial advice. We owe it to God, to His reputation and to the spread of His glory and the gospel around the world to be smart, savvy, clever and sharp when it comes to making money count.

In this section, we'll look at the following areas: (1) the significance of dreaming large; (2) whether or not it is right to expect a return on our investments; (3) what Lydia teaches us; (4) the difference between business and profession; (5) the consequences of our generation's mismanagement of money on our children's generation; and (6) the role God plays in it all.

CHAPTER 14

Dream Large!

Dreaming large has the power to move the heart of God! A big part of success is first having a vision and a dream to guide your steps. Our God has the power to bring big dreams to pass. Dreaming large gives people something to aim for and inspires others to dream large, too.

The seed for the dream and vision for our church owning the former home of the Los Angeles Lakers basketball team began more than 25 years ago. I sat on the third row from the back at Garden Grove Community Church pastored by Dr. Robert Schuller, which would later become the Crystal Cathedral. I sat there in the early days of that ministry and looked around, wrestling with a question I would revisit several times in the future.

I saw all that God was doing—and wondered if God was prejudiced! Really! That thought crossed my mind several times. I saw the big vision Dr. Schuller had, and he'd not even broken ground on the magnificent Crystal Cathedral yet. I was freaked out when a whole wall of the building opened like drapes and Dr. Schuller began preaching, not only to those of us in the sanctuary but to hundreds outside, with portable speakers on their car windows like at a drive-in theatre! I thought, *You go, man!* God used Dr. Schuller to lift my eyes beyond the plush grounds of the Garden Grove church.

I went back on several occasions and as I listened, I learned that the key to what I saw was the power of a big God who inspires big dreams. I saw this principle again in the life of a great man of faith who later became a dear friend, Dr. Frederick K. C. Price. I watched the Lord use his faith to build a 10,000-seat dome in the heart of the ghetto of Los Angeles! As an impressionable young minister, I said again, "You go, man!" But when I began to realize the power of faith and the power of the God of my faith, when I began to realize the power of big dreams and the power of the big God who inspires big dreams, I started saying, "You go, God!"

I am still startled when people tell me how amazed they are at what Faithful Central Bible Church is doing. I guess I have been so close to the journey that I don't take time to view it from the perspective of observers. Believe it or not, it's my fellow preachers who give me the most flack and criticism, and who grill me relentlessly about the fact that Faithful Central now owns the former home of the mighty Los Angeles Lakers! I constantly have to remind them: It is God who took us on a path from being a 350-member congregation to some 14,000 members! I fear that my response might sound pious and super-spiritual, but the truth is, we are simply following God's process. And we are doing it because He is calling our church to accomplish mighty things in this generation.

If you've got a big God, then you can trust Him to do big works! Dream large! God can handle it. Dreaming big causes a person to be on the lookout for viable business and financial opportunities.

When we move into the world of business, we need to learn how to talk world talk and keep a heavenly head. We need to keep our spirits true to God but know how to maneuver and talk and negotiate and discuss intelligently in the world, because this is the world where we have to live and operate. If you can't talk money talk on a high level, make sure you surround yourself with a team that can.

In the early years, I would often sit in meetings where the agenda was millions and millions of dollars—and I would sit there not knowing what to say. Sometimes I didn't even understand the questions being asked, let alone the answers! But I had sharp, talented people around me and if I couldn't make it, I'd let the smart folk do the talking! I developed the skill of looking and sounding intelligent when in fact I didn't have the foggiest idea what was going on. I was there by the grace of God, I was there not knowing all the questions nor the answers, I was there sometimes not knowing why or how I got there–*but I was there!* Like Mephibosheth, I had a handicap, but I was still at the table (see 2 Sam. 9:13).

God will grant you favor with people in financial industries because it takes money to build God's kingdom on Earth. He will bless those relationships, such as the ones we initiated back when Faithful Central Bible Church set out to purchase the Great Western Forum. Initially, some of the financial experts we sought out weren't so sure about what we had in mind. In the beginning of our quest, they didn't quite catch the fire of our dream. But when the idea caught on with them, they began to say, "Pastor, we are going to do this!" Some of those professional business and financial advisers weren't even Christians at the time, but as they saw what God was doing, some of the very same financial experts who advised us during the deal became our fellow believers to the glory of God!

Most people dream too small. If you learn how big our God is, it will greatly impact the size of your dreams.

Understanding the Dimensions of God

Scottish reformer John Knox once said, "A man with God is always in the majority."[1] If we can ever begin to fully understand the dimensions of our God, it will enlarge the dimensions of our dreams. *God is big!* He is able to effect more than we could ever imagine. If we can wrap our mind around how great He is, we will be able to see how much He can do for us.

Begin to think differently! Stop dreaming small. If others try to discourage you, don't back off—stick to your vision and walk on. God is calling us to a whole new level, a whole new dimension, a whole new arena.

Much of the criticism I've experienced so far with regard to Faithful Central Bible Church's growth over the past quarter of a century has been from other churches that don't seem to want to dream big enough to step out of the boat and trust the Lord to keep them from sinking. God told us to come with Him. When He commands you to do something, have faith enough to do it and watch the miracles begin!

> "Come," [Jesus] said. Then Peter got down out of the boat, walked on the water and came toward Jesus (Matt. 14:29, *NIV*).

Can you imagine if Peter had stayed in the boat when Jesus said, "Come"? If Peter had said, "No, no—not me, Lord. I ain't comin' out there, all stormy and wet and rainy like this, no siree! I'm gonna stay right here nice and comfortable in the boat, thanks." He would have missed out on a blessing that only *one man in human history* got to tell his grandkids about! Peter walked on water! In a storm! *With Jesus!* Why? Because Jesus said, "Come" and Peter climbed out of the boat and came!

Don't ever be afraid to get out of the boat. Don't back off your dream just because other people can't see it like you do. Don't lose vision because other folk can't see what you see. That's why God gave *you* the vision. He wanted somebody who could see the unseeable, who could touch the intangible, who could do the impossible. If you're willing to get out of the boat and trust God, you can walk on water! (But first you have to get out of the boat!)

Deepwater Blessings

Those who go down to the sea in ships, who do business in great waters, they see the works of the LORD, and His wonders in the deep.

PSALM 107:23-24

The verse above is a nautical metaphor of people who do business as fishermen. The implication of the text is that there are those "holy bold" people who launch out into the deep to do business, in contrast to those who stay safe in the shallows.

Notice that it's only those who "do business in great waters" who will "see the works of the Lord, and His wonders in the deep." If you want deepwater blessings, be willing to go deep. Sure, there are some fish in the shallow waters. You've got your guppies and your anchovies and your minnows. But there are some real *fish* in the deep water! You can do some business by the seashore, but the few who have enough vision, who have enough foresight, who sometimes are just crazy enough to get into a ship and venture out into the great waters and are willing to step out of the boat in faith when they get there—*those* are the people who are going to accomplish great things that can't even be imagined back yonder in the shallows.

Don't expect to receive deepwater blessings by living a shallow-water life. God cannot fit whale-sized blessings into a cute little goldfish bowl. I know your goldfish bowl is cute. You got some teeny little goldfish splashing around in there all cute and gold, but you cannot fit God-sized blessings into that bowl. I once heard something interesting about a goldfish: The size of a goldfish is determined by the size of its container. I was told that if you put a goldfish into a small goldfish bowl, that little goldfish will grow to be maybe an inch or two long. But if you take that very same goldfish out and put it into a great big pond, there's no telling how big that goldfish will get now that it has some breathing room and can swim like it has never swum before! Get out of your little bowl! We serve a God who promises that if we keep Him first and foremost in all things, He'll pour us out blessings so big that we will have no room to receive them!

Once you make up your mind that you will trust God in deep water, you realize that you've signed up for a deep-faith swim—when you only paddle near the shore and the winds kick up and the waves turn the boat over, you can just stand up and walk back home! Where's the faith in that? On the other hand, when you're out there in deep water and the boat starts reeling and rocking and the storms of life begin tossing and turning and you get thrown out of the boat, there's nothing to hold you up but the mighty hand of God. And personally, I would rather be in God's hand in deep water than in my own hands standing by the shore, splashing with the minnows.

Those who go down to the sea in ships to do business in great waters—those are the ones who see the wonders of the Lord and His miracles in the deep.

Are you trusting God to do something that no one else can do so that when He does it you'll know exactly who did it? What are you believing God for? Is it big? Or are you stuck in the shallows? Let's get specific: *What is your vision for your life?* Where do you plan to be in four years? Ten years? What kind of plan do you have for your children? For your family? For your career? For your finances? How far down the road can you see? And how far are you trusting God *beyond* where you can see?

I challenge you to venture into the deep and begin to experience His deepwater blessings!

Great Dreams in Progress

Over the past several years, Faithful Central Bible Church has traveled into some waters that are deeper than we've ever been in before. And let me tell you, we are seeing some amazing blessings there. Faithful Central's building project is doing serious damage to the kingdom of darkness.

For example, there are so few places in our city where young people can go and just have a good time in healthy ways. That is a void we have been called to fill, and we are filling it! We are providing a place for people to come and enjoy themselves, a place where they can experience good, wholesome fun. It's okay to be saved *and* have fun! I get nervous in places where it's heavy all the time. I like the anointing, but it's okay to laugh in our church.

How is your joy of salvation? How deep is your joy in the Lord? There's a Jesus joy that comes from deep on the inside that's based on our relationship with God. It assures us that we're on our way to heaven and that we can enjoy our journey along the way!

There are theological and biblical principles to what we are doing. When God says to go in and posses the land, go in and take over! Before we could travel into the deep waters with our church building project, we had to dream big first. It was a dream that came from God, a dream that encouraged us, inspired us, gave us a vision and a drive. That is what dreams do. Dreams put you on the right path and prod you to keep going every step of the way. But in order to keep going, you first have to *get going*! Don't fall into the trap of just dreaming all the time–act on your dreams. Make them happen! Bring them to reality. Remember: Thought creates! Get this information, this knowledge, into your spirit and start thinking about how to take God's process and bring your vision to life.

Process is the engine that launches your dreams into reality. Process puts wind to the sails of your visions and ideas. Once you start following through and acting on your dreams, people will be amazed. Time will prove to them that you're on the right track, that your dreams weren't all that crazy; they just required a big God to bring them to reality! What a testimony—you'll have an opportunity to point people to the *real* Master of business administration!

Don't get discouraged. Your dreams won't come to pass instantly, but as you work alongside God to bring your dreams to life, they will take off and soar. Never let go of your vision just because others can't see it. It is *your* vision. *Live it!*

By knowledge the rooms are filled with all precious and pleasant riches.

PROVERBS 24:4

Note

1. John Knox (1513–1572), inscription on the Reformation Monument, Geneva, Switzerland.

Chapter 15

Expect a Return

All that is in Heaven and in earth is Yours;
yours is the kingdom, O Lord, and You are exalted as head over all.
1 Chronicles 29:11

At Christmastime when I was growing up, my mother would stand in front of us kids and give us money, telling us to go buy gifts for our family members and friends for Christmas. So we kids would take the money and go on a shopping spree for everyone. When Christmas day came and we were all opening gifts, our mother would act surprised at receiving her gifts. She knew where the money came from—it came from her!—but still she pretended to be surprised. She was genuinely happy with the gifts, even though she was the source of the money for buying them.

One Christmas when I got money from my mother to purchase gifts, I happened to have a new girlfriend and I got a little carried away buying gifts. Christmas day rolled around, and I will never forget the look on my mother's face that morning. I had spent all my money on my girlfriend! Not a cent on anyone else, not even my mom—even though *she* was the one who had given me money in the first place! When all the gifts were given out, she looked at me with a look that didn't need words. *Where's mine?* her pained expression said. Let me tell you, I will never forget how hurt she was by what I did to her—worse, by what I *didn't do* for her. She had given me the money with which I was to have blessed others, and I spent it all on my selfish desire, completely forgetting the source.

The same principle holds true with our relationship to God. He is the One who provides our all, yet He's still pleased when He receives back from us, His children. When we throw His money away on other things, He is rightfully hurt, just like my mother was when I spent all the money she gave me on my girlfriend. She expected a little something . . . and got nothing. She had every right to want something—she gave the money out of love for me, her son.

Receivers by Nature

Human beings are receivers by nature. We don't naturally give. It's ingrained into us from birth to *want*, to *get*, to *receive*. You don't see too many babies who quietly, patiently wait to be fed or have their diapers changed. They holler!

A child's natural instinct is to take and to receive—parents have to teach their children to share because their nature is to be possessive. How many two-year-olds say, "Hi, Mom. How can I help you today? Vacuum the floors? Dust the furniture? Cup of coffee?" No—they want toys to play with and another cup of juice, and it all better be while *Dora the Explorer* is clamoring in the background on a nearby TV! Teenagers are even less prone to altruistic giving. As we get older, the approach and subtleties change, but we still want, want, want.

Christians who are afraid to expect a return are probably reacting to this natural human tendency to *want*. They realize this inclination in themselves and others and they go to the opposite extreme, thinking that receiving is bad. But it's not, as long as our attitudes and motives are pure.

However, humans have to be trained to initiate selfless giving. This training begins with the understanding that we came into the world with nothing and that everything we have is a gift to us from a Father who gives to us not because He has to, but because He loves us. Once we grasp that understanding, it makes giving easier to initiate.

God is a natural giver. And as much as you wouldn't want someone to reject a gift you give them, God doesn't want us to refuse His gifts. Once we receive those gifts, however, we have to be ready to be givers ourselves, to follow God's pattern. It's a continual, ongoing cycle. God gives. We receive. We take what we receive and give to others. They take what they've received and hopefully give it back to God's purposes. And the process keeps going. But in order for the process to work, we have to be willing to be givers. This can be hard because giving doesn't come naturally. We have to be trained, our minds renewed for that activity. It takes a degree of conscious reprogramming to get our hearts and minds to *want* to give. But it can be done: God set the example!

Obedient Giving

If you ask most people about the relationship between giving and receiving, they'll probably tell you that they're opposites. I'd like to challenge that thinking: Giving and receiving are *not* antithetical to one another. Giving and receiving are not separate, individual functions—they're two sides of the same coin. What we give to God is what we have already received from Him, and what He gives us to oversee, we must submit back in His direction. Understanding this is essential to the Christian, because it impacts all that we do—how we give the tithe, how we trust God to provide and even how we approach salvation.

It Started with God . . .

For God so loved the world that He gave His only begotten Son, that whoever believes in Him should not perish but have everlasting life.

JOHN 3:16

Giving began with God. He set the supreme pattern for giving. In fact, God was not only the first one to give—He had to *create* something to give. In the beginning, He created the heavens and the Earth, and then He began to give. God made the sun, which gives heat and sustains life. God made the moon, which exerts its gravitational pull on the oceans to create the tides that circulate the great waters. God made the air, which gives by keeping us alive. God made the earth, which gives of its abundance for our sustenance. God made the sea, which gives. Everything God made gives.

God's ultimate act of giving was the gift of His Son, Jesus, and Jesus gave His very life. The familiar text of John 3:16 tells us that God loved the world so much that He gave what was of the utmost and precious value to Him. This action of God's giving His Son came with two obvious gifts for us: not perishing *and* receiving eternal life. And then, for those who accept the gift of Jesus, a *third* gift is given:

> As many as received Him, to them *He gave the right to become children of God*, to those who believe in His name: who were born, not of blood, nor of the will of the flesh, nor of the will of man, but of God (John 1:12-13, emphasis added).

The third gift is that those who believe in Jesus and accept the gift of salvation (along with its dual gifts of not perishing and enjoying eternal life) become children of God. What God gets in the transaction is that by *giving* His Son, He *receives* new sons and daughters. God's desire is that everyone should become His children, and to bring that about, He sacrificed Jesus. In other words, He gave the One to receive the many.

God gave, *expecting* to receive something in return. He knew that the "investment" of His Son would yield the result of new children to share eternal relationship with—*that* is why He gave. He sent His only

Son, expecting to get a return on His investment. It was a steep investment, but it paid off, yielding a deep return.

From the very start, God got a great return. He got Matthew, Mark, Luke, Peter, James, Paul and all the other apostles and disciples. And as they spread the gospel, others were added to His kingdom—and it keeps getting bigger and broader and better as time marches on.

God's investment reveals that giving and receiving are actually one ongoing, revolving spiritual activity, yielding stronger and stronger returns.

True to His Word

Once we realize that God gave Christ expecting a return, it opens up a whole new dimension of understanding on the topic of receiving: It's alright for us to expect a return on our investments. In fact, God Himself set the pattern when He said:

> Give, and it will be given to you: good measure, pressed down, shaken together, and running over will be put into your bosom. For with the same measure that you use, it will be measured back to you (Luke 6:38).

Many people think it's somehow unspiritual to expect a return when they give, but that mind-set basically says that it's wrong to trust God's own example. This doesn't mean that your motive to give should be that you'll get a return. No—it means that it's okay simply to know that you one day will. God Himself is the One who said that when we give, it will be given back to us—and in *abundance*!

Giving requires faith that God will be true to His word. A spiritual giver who gives in faith can expect to be blessed. Yet, some people still don't feel comfortable going around thinking that that is what should happen. They feel like that's setting an impure motive for giving—and they're right *if* that's the motive for giving. But as long as your motive is pure and selfless in the first place, you *can* go expecting something to happen. You might not know when or where or how, but it's going to be given back to you, in good measure *and running over*.

What we receive may not be huge piles of cash—that's not what God promises. In fact, God doesn't specify *what* we'll receive. It could be money, it could be other things, it could be a combination. But what He does say is that we'll receive something of value and that it will be in abundance. Your abundant return might be in the form of a promotion. It might be in the form of a new job. It might be in the form of a raise. It could even be a gift. An inheritance. A good return on a financial investment. But the fact remains that you *will* get a return and it *will* be abundant. That's simply God's pattern.

Abundance is like when your trash can is full and you don't want to take it out to the curb or to the garage, so you just put your foot into it and push it down so that you can cram more stuff into it. That's a picture of God's abundant return to us. Pressed down, shaken together and running over—and God doesn't give garbage!

CHAPTER 16

The Lesson of Lydia

And on the Sabbath day we went out of the city to the riverside,
where prayer was customarily made;
and we sat down and spoke to the women who met there.
Now a certain woman named Lydia heard us.
She was a seller of purple from the city of Thyatira, who worshiped God.

ACTS 16:13-14

Acts 16:10 begins what is called the "we" section of the book of Acts. Prior to this account, because Luke was not part of Paul's entourage, he wrote in the third person. In Acts 16:10, however, Luke shifts from third-person plural to first-person plural—from "them" and "they" to "us" and "we." From this passage forward, throughout the rest of the book of Acts, Luke writes from the perspective of an eyewitness involved in the events he recounts. No longer is he on the outside looking in—he is now involved in the action.

Lydia

Luke recounts their arrival in a city called Philippi. Just outside town they went to the riverside, where they met a group of women who gathered there regularly for prayer. Included in this group was a woman named Lydia, who is identified as a seller of purple (one version says "of dyed fabrics").

Purple cloth was highly valued and very expensive in that day. It was commonly worn by royalty, noblemen and Roman senators as a public sign of their high position. One reason for the high cost of the purple fabrics was the labor-intensive nature of production. The dye used to create the deep, rich hues came from mollusks, which were white inside and turned to a deep crimson shade when exposed to sunlight.

Outside sources suggest that as a seller of the expensive purple cloth, Lydia was most likely a successful and wealthy businesswoman, and Scripture indicates the same. Acts 16:15 refers to "members of her household" (*NIV*), indicating that she may have had servants and relatives living with her.

Lydia lived in the town of Thyatira, which was on the main route between Pergamus and Sardis. It was not a port town like some of the other commercial cities of the region—it was slightly inland on a major trade route. Thyatira was known for its guilds. In our economy, guilds would be like unions or trade societies. Many anthropological and historical artifacts have been excavated from Thyatira that reveal the actual names of some of these various guilds. The most prominent guild in Thyatira at the time was a union comprised of people who worked with dyes and fabrics. It was what we might today refer to as a fabric-makers union. As a seller of dyes, fabrics and dyed fabrics in and around the area of Sardis (primarily to the tradesmen who came through that route), Lydia was likely a member of this fabric-makers guild.

Thyatira was also a pagan city. In fact, it was the home of many pagan shrines and temples, including a shrine to an idol god called Tyrimnos. The temple to Tyrimnos was one of the central architectural features of Thyatira. There were also many other shrines and smaller temples to foreign idols and gods, including a shrine to a woman named Jezebel, who called herself a prophetess (mentioned in Revelation 2:20). Thus, Thyatira was not exactly what you'd call a holy city.

Acts tells us that Lydia worshiped the God of the Hebrews, the God of Israel. And now, she was about to hear of Jesus . . .

> Lydia worshipped God. The Lord opened her heart to heed the things spoken by Paul (Acts 16:14).

Although she lived in a city known for its sinners and idol worshipers, Lydia was faithful to the kingdom of God. In talking to her and the others there at the riverside about his personal testimony, Paul more than likely told them that he was a former Pharisee and strict enforcer of Jewish law, and about his encounter with Jesus on the road to Damascus and his subsequent conversion to Christianity. Paul told them that this Jesus of Nazareth was indeed the long-awaited *Mashiyach*, or Messiah, foretold in the Jewish Torah. He explained that Jesus Messiah had come, fulfilling prophecy, and in accordance with prophecy, had been crucified in order to stand in as the ultimate sacrifice for the sins of mankind. Then, after rising from the dead as foretold by the prophet Isaiah, Jesus had appeared to the disciples and ascended to the right hand of God in heaven.

This news was probably far beyond anything Lydia had ever been taught before. But the Lord opened her heart to accept Paul's message, and she responded immediately to his teaching of the Gospel and to the urging of the Holy Spirit by accepting Jesus as the Christ, Messiah. Acts 16 says that Lydia was found faithful, and that Paul and company stayed with her and baptized her. Ultimately, as told in Acts 16:40, Lydia's house became a place of worship and the birthplace of the church in Philippi.

The story of Lydia is powerful, with myriad implications and lessons! She was a believer who made her money doing business in a place of idolatry, wickedness, sinners, sexual immorality and unrighteousness—and yet *remained faithful*! What an example. Her heart, her actions, her choices, her activities, gave her honorable mention in the Scriptures for eternity.

Not *Where* but *Whether*

An important lesson we take from the story of Lydia has to do with her approach to worship. She was not constrained by tradition. Lydia realized that *whether* she worshiped was more important than *where* she worshiped.

The Bible says that Lydia and the women customarily gathered at the riverside for prayer. The Bible does not say that the women gathered *inside* the city for prayer—they gathered *outside* of the city, which means they were off the regular path. They gathered down by the riverside. Not in a synagogue, temple or *shul*. Not in a customary or a traditional holy place of worship. They gathered by the riverside, a very unorthodox place to pray.

When people join together for prayer, they communicate with God. *Prayer* means that we enter into the presence of the living God. In prayer, we can praise God. In prayer, we can worship God. These women met by the river in order to meet with God and pray together, and possibly also to talk business. They met in a place that was not the usual, consecrated, specially designated holy place. In fact, it might have been a place near a little river beach, where folk normally gathered to have recreational fun. And it was there, in this place, that a group of saints got together to have a prayer meeting and get in touch with *Eohiym*, God of Israel.

The point is this: The "Lydia women" found a praying ground where folk did not usually gather to pray. If we are going to be what God has called us to be, we've got to get to the point where we are able to go beyond the traditional holy places of worship. We cannot limit ourselves to stay behind stained-glass windows and sit in padded pews and be surrounded by precious icons on holy walls. We must get to the point where it is not all about the *place* we worship but *whether* we worship. Whether we are making the effort to get in touch with God. Whether we've made the commitment to Him. Whether we *pray*—no matter if we can find a synagogue or a temple or a church to pray in or not.

It doesn't matter if your church, your Bible group, your prayer gathering, meets close to a cemetery, next to a casino, by a gambling hall or smack dab in the middle of a ghetto. Once you make up your mind that it's not about *where* you are, but about *who* you are and *whether* you are, then you can be sanctified and set aside and consecrated to God's work.

If we don't approach worship with the same open-mindedness that Lydia did, we'll miss out. Don't get caught up in what's around you when you meet to pray to God. Make up your mind that you're not going to let anybody or anything or any sign or any reputation or any past history stop you from doing what God has called you to do. Meet up with God by your "riverside," even if there is nobody there but you and God. You have too much to praise Him for, too much to thank Him for, and you don't have time to look around and make sure there's stained glass in the window, a sign on the door, a cross bolted to a wall, and a painting of Jesus above the altar. Just praise Him wherever you are!

When I think about the goodness of Jesus and all that He's done for me, my soul can cry out down by the river, cry out in the Houston Astrodome, cry out in the Great Western Forum, cry out driving down the expressway, cry out all by myself! Because you don't know like I know what the Lord has done for me!

Don't listen to people who say, "Well, you know, I can't worship in there." These women met God by the riverside! What if you were there on that day when Jesus fed the 5,000 and you said, "I can't handle the crowd. I'll sit this one out." You can't gather by the Sea of Galilee with Jesus? You have to meet only in your church? You would have missed lunch with the Lord of the universe that day if you're the type who worries about the place and the crowd!

Lydia's Priorities

Some people claim that the Bible condemns money. It quite obviously does not. The Word clearly says in 1 Timothy 6:10, that it's "the love of money" that is a root of all kinds of evil—not the money itself. It's all about priorities, attitude and motive.

There was once a wealthy man whom Jesus called out on the issue of loving money more than Him:

> As He was going out on the road, one came running, knelt before Him, and asked Him, "Good Teacher, what shall I do that I may inherit eternal life?"
>
> So Jesus said to him, "Why do you call Me good? No one is good but One, that is, God. You know the commandments: 'Do not commit adultery,' 'Do not murder,' 'Do not steal,' 'Do not bear false witness,' 'Do not defraud,' 'Honor your father and your mother.'"
>
> And he answered and said to Him, "Teacher, all these things I have kept from my youth."
>
> Then Jesus, looking at him, loved him, and said to him, "One thing you lack: Go your way, sell whatever you have and give to the poor, and you will have treasure in Heaven; and come, take up the cross, and follow Me."
>
> But he was sad at this word, and went away sorrowful, for he had great possessions (Mark 10:17-22).

The man asked Jesus what he must do to make it to heaven, and Jesus told him to take all of his riches, convert them back to money and give it to the needy, and then start living his life for Him. But the man walked away sorrowful, because he was rich and thought he was being told to give away what he took to be *his* money and become poor. That's not what Jesus was requesting.

The danger of the enemy's attack about abundance is that he will make us trust in our riches, our investments and our portfolio more than in God. This man's aim with his money was not to do God's will with what God had given him. His priority instead was to hoard it for himself and to not honor its Source (God) by changing his attitude and using money to God's purpose and glory. He didn't want to share with the poor, didn't want to follow Jesus, and didn't want to even acknowledge that it was God who had allowed him to amass his wealth. Satan loves that attitude.

This is why the story of Lydia is such a great example for us. We know she was wealthy, yet she kept her priorities straight and clearly loved God above all else. She had money, yet she did not "love" it or place it above God. She maintained her testimony while living in a sin-riddled city surrounded by blasphemers, sinners and rejecters of God. As a matter of fact, in Revelation 2 we read that even some of the *believers* in Thyatira were living just like the sinners in the world! And they were called on the carpet by God:

> Nevertheless I have a few things against you, because you allow that woman Jezebel, who calls herself a prophetess, to teach and seduce My servants to commit sexual immorality and eat things sacrificed to idols. And I gave her time to repent of her sexual immorality, and she did not repent (Rev. 2:20-21).

Yet living here in the middle of this same city was a woman who believed in God, was successful and rich *and* was singled out as a positive example in the Bible for all generations. If Lydia could do all that—

build a business, open her house to a church, gain wealth, maintain her spiritual and moral integrity, and honor God—can't we? We should at least strive for that. It's the best of the best!

CHAPTER 17

The Difference Between Business and Profession

Then Jesus said to them, "Follow Me, and I will make you become fishers of men."

MARK 1:17

Lydia is proof of an important lesson that we all need to learn: The difference between one's profession and one's business. Profession and business are two different things. Lydia's profession was selling dyed fabric, but her *business* was Kingdom business.

The Difference

Your *profession* is what you do on the surface. Your *business* is the underlying, motivating cause that gives true meaning and value to your life. If you are a doctor, for instance, your *profession* is being a physician, but your *business* is helping people and making them well—as a business, that's your ultimate goal.

Sometimes business is an intangible; sometimes it's not. In some cases a profession and a business might be completely different. Your profession might support your business, though what is seen visibly through your profession might not directly indicate exactly what your business is. Take for example the holder of the most individual high-value lots of real estate in the world. It's not Donald Trump. Not Leona Helmsley. Not the Queen of England. It's not even the U.S. government. It's the McDonald's Corporation. That's correct, the fast food restaurant chain. McDonald's owns more high-visibility real estate than even the Catholic Church. Probably only Starbucks gives McDonald's serious competition for the title!

Legend has it that at a meeting after a lecture he once gave at North Carolina University, Ray Kroc, founder of McDonald's, asked the students what business he was in. Of course they chuckled and snickered and said, "Mickey Dees! You're in the burger biz!"

According to the legend, Mr. Kroc smiled and said, "No. You missed it. I'm in the *real estate business*." Huh?? That's right, not *the all-meat patties on a sesame-seed bun* business, but the *real estate business.* Mr. Kroc explained that his stores are located in the highest traffic, highest exposure areas in most major cities the world over, giving McDonald's ownership of prime real estate around the globe. The McDonald's Corporation began to realize a few years after they started growing in the hamburger business that they were not just acquiring stores to flip burgers, but they were also acquiring real estate.

The McDonald's Corporation perfectly illustrates the distinction between business and profession. Their *profession* was selling hamburgers—their *business* was real estate. Other examples display this simple differentiation between profession and business:

Lydia

Profession	Selling dyed purple fabric
Business	*Kingdom business: providing a place for a local church, disseminating the Word of God, giving a place of comfort and safety to the people of God*

Matthew

Profession	Collecting taxes
Business	*Kingdom business: following Jesus Christ as a disciple, recording and writing the Gospel of Matthew*

Jesus	
Profession	Carpentry, before becoming a rabbi full-time, which, by Jewish law, could only happen after a man turned 30
Business:	*Kingdom business: "I must be about My Father's business" (Luke 2:49)*

James and John	
Profession	Fishing
Business:	*Kingdom business: being fishers of men*

Does It Matter?

Does understanding the difference between business and profession really matter all that much? Absolutely. Once we get this straight in our thinking as Christians in our efforts to take care of business using God's process, we are ready to be fully effective in His kingdom—then we realize that we can be about God's business no matter what our profession.

Faithful Central Bible Church is a sports arena owner-operator. Although our profession has extended to include real estate ventures and sports arena operations, we have not lost sight of our business: *expanding God's kingdom*. Until we purchased the Great Western Forum, there was no sports arena in the world owned by a church. When we decided to buy this historic sports landmark, our bank didn't understand it. They thought we were just trying to buy a bigger building for our growing church family. We explained to them, Yes, we're doing that *... and then some!* We operate the arena as a business during times when the church isn't meeting. Although our profession is being an arena owner-operator, our business is still Kingdom business. While competitors are in the arena trying to score points for and against the home team, we're watching Jesus do slam-dunks on the devil and scoring points for Team Heaven!

Our profession may be running a large entertainment arena in Los Angeles, but our business is still Kingdom business.

Our business is *changing lives.*

Our business is *giving to the community.*

Our business is *teaching and encouraging young people to dare to dream as big as our God.*

Our business is *generating jobs.*

Our business is *touching souls and taking the Kingdom where no church has dared to go before.*

Our business is *inspiring people not just to super-size their thinking, but to God-size it!*

What great businesses to be in!

What's your business? Don't say, "Oh, I'm a salesperson."

"I'm a lawyer."

"I'm a doctor."

"I'm a mechanic."

That's your *profession*. I'm talking about your *business*—the purpose and deeper meaning and motivation behind your profession. Are you expanding the Kingdom? Are you making a living or building a life? Are you a reservoir of resources or a channel of compassion?

If you're not sure what your business is, I'd like to suggest that you refocus your point of view and start expanding God's kingdom on Earth, no matter what your profession is. Get into a mind-set of Kingdom business and watch God go to work in your life!

Chapter 18

A Generation on the Brink

Too many of our children today are not being taught a solid biblical understanding of money. Consequently, they are entering adulthood spiritually uninformed and financially untrained. Perhaps it's because their parents don't comprehend dealing with monetary matters.

Children watch as their parents get charge accounts at jewelry stores, department stores, clothing stores and online stores, and the purpose is always the same: to buy more *stuff* with money they don't have. This leads their children's value systems to get all out of whack. Once *they* get money, they don't know how to handle it either. As they grow up to be adults, they set the same poor example for the generation after them and the cycle will worsen. Instead of investing money, they'll wear it around their necks, put it into new cars, wear it on their fingers, drape it on their bodies, shove it into DVD players and listen to it through earphones. All because our generation is not teaching them to handle their financial affairs God's way.

As blessings from God, our children are assets in themselves. It is our responsibility to train them up in God's ways so that they are financially and morally prepared to properly deal with the life ahead of them. This includes biblical instructions for handling money God's way. It is urgent that we adults get our own money matters ironed out, because taking care of business properly and wisely doesn't affect only us, it affects the next generation as well.

The very same thing that is occurring with our generation as parents and with our children today was also happening over 2,400 years ago, as the passage below depicts:

> Others were saying, "We are mortgaging our fields, our vineyards and our homes to get grain during the famine." Still others were saying, "We have had to borrow money to pay the king's tax on our fields and vineyards. Although we are of the same flesh and blood as our countrymen and though our sons are as good as theirs, yet we have to subject our sons and daughters to slavery. Some of our daughters have already been enslaved, but we are powerless, because our fields and our vineyards belong to others" (Neh. 5:3-5, *NIV*).

The generation being raised by today's so-called "baby boomers" is in bondage. It is said that this will be the first American generation that has not done better economically than the one that preceded it.

What kind of legacy are we leaving our children? Everything that we do and don't do has a trickle-down effect to the next generation and beyond. The consequences of our actions will reverberate into future generations. Right now we have a generation being lead into slavery because the previous generation is not handling finances properly, nor are we teaching our children biblical tenets of money management. We're not operating in a mind-set of productivity, nor are we passing these scriptural teachings on to our children. This negligence trickles down, growing stickier, like a thick sludge, onto the next generation. And the next, and the next.

By the time our grandchildren enter their 20s, our children will be so far in bondage that they'll have no inheritance to leave them. Just as in Nehemiah's time, they'll have to borrow money just to pay their taxes to the government. If we don't reverse this alarming trend, our grandchildren will have no choice but to go into financial bondage to pay off their parents' debts and loans and credit card bills and taxes—all because our generation was negligent in teaching our children sound money management.

We can talk about how many members we have in our churches and how much money we have in our accounts and how much the budget is, but if we don't have something to pass on to the next generation that goes beyond bricks and mortar, we've missed God's teaching and have made things far more financially difficult for our kids.

God gave us a clear process that will help our children to be what God has called them to be. It is up to us to teach it to them, to take them beyond the way things used to be. We've got to teach them that there is something more than TV shows containing violent men, scantily clad women, the newest clothing fads, iPods, podcasts, promiscuous sex, violent video games, and on and on to destructive infinitum.

There are geniuses in the streets of America's inner cities who are wearing street gang colors and throwing gang signs. There are mental giants with tremendous ability to lead and motivate people. There are minds out on the streets that have taken wayward boys and girls whose parents don't have time for them and organized them into criminal gangs run as tightly as any Fortune 500 corporation. During attempts to broker peace agreements between rival gangs in Los Angeles, my friend Steve Harvey and I learned and discussed how brilliant some of these street warriors are. Some of these guys have genius minds. There are kids on the streets who are undirected and brilliant, whose energies have been programmed and directed in the wrong ways. If the Church can't save them, who can? How can we turn them around if we're giving them no lasting models or wise teachings? When will we offer them better examples than what the world is offering?

This generation is in jeopardy because we are not training them. In fact, by not teaching them biblical tenets, *we* are helping to place them into bondage. We have a generation of young people who can see no further than *right here* and *right now*. Their value system and priorities are no further than what is in front of them, because they aren't being taught any better. This stunts their psychological growth and morphs their self-image into something indefinable. They believe their value comes from what they wear and how many diamonds are on their fingers and how cool they look and how many songs their iPod holds, instead of virtue and character and good morals and following the heart of the Master.

This generation is dangling on the edge. Our children are being raised by media images that the world claims represent "the best." Bling-bling. Credit card debt (the highest average balance due in the entire world). Money borrowed for brand-new cars (which lose nearly half their value in the first few months—and you still owe the full amount plus interest). No-down, interest-only mortgages (buy today, pay tomorrow). For some, the only people they see paying cash for cars are pimps and drug dealers. This generation will pay tomorrow alright. And tomorrow is already knocking.

If we don't change all that, we'll lose this teen and 20-something generation *and* the generation that'll come from their loins, our grandchildren.

> Train up a child in the way he should go, and when he is old he will not depart from it (Prov. 22:6).

We *can* reverse the situation and make sure that our kids are equipped for success. But a reprogramming is necessary if this generation coming up is going to have half a chance to be better people and to leave better legacies than sex and war and "pimp my ride" and who looks best and who wears less.

There are people out there who could run successful corporations if we will make an effort to reprogram their mind-set and teach them to channel that energy into something positive. Is your church doing that? Are they teaching principles to their children that will attract a generation beyond them to do things God's way? This generation has the potential to be the greatest generation for God *ever*!

And it's all in our hands. As adults, we have a *responsibility* to train and instruct our children in the fear and admonition of the Lord, which include spiritual matters *and* money matters. How we do this makes all the difference. If we want to successfully instruct them, we must set examples. It doesn't work to simply *tell* our children—we must *show* them. We must state with confidence, "Do as I say *and* as I do."

The Bible says an entire *generation* went into slavery and bondage because the previous generation had messed it all up for them. It shall not be so on my watch! It shall not be so in my house! It shall not be so with the generation of kids who sing in our church on Sundays! They shall see something different. They shall dream bigger dreams. They shall set their sights higher. They shall know the value that God places on them. An entire generation is at stake.

> The good leave an inheritance to their children's children (Prov. 13:22, *NRSV*).

Note in the Scripture above that it is the "good" who leave an inheritance for their grandchildren. That's the pattern: If you're good, you'll leave something for your grandkids. The implication is that if you're not a good person, then you won't. In order to leave an inheritance, you have to build, create, make something. In order to do that, you have to learn how. God teaches us how, in His process for money management.

The word "inheritance" (*nachal* in Hebrew) has to do with occupancy, as in a place or something to be occupied. When God says to leave to our children's children an inheritance, it means we are to leave them *space* to occupy. It refers to land that is divided. We've already learned that God owns all the land. In Bible times, wealth was measured largely by land owned. We can understand this in today's economic terms as passing on to our children something of financial value, whether it's land or other tangible assets. Thus, "the good leave an inheritance" signifies a space, a place, land to be occupied by the children of our children. Taking a big-picture perspective, this doesn't apply only to the physical—it also applies to spiritual teachings we leave behind for our children.

Our Children's Children

The inheritance we leave behind is not just for our children, but it's for *their* children as well, and on down the line throughout the generations. What we pass on to our children should be both spiritual and practical.

Spiritual: When the time comes time for your children to instruct and train their own children, they will be able to draw on the spiritual side of the financial lessons you've taught them. What you teach them from a biblical perspective today is an investment in the training and well-being of generations to come from them.

Practical: In addition to leaving a worthwhile, sustainable inheritance that will have long-lasting value, you also need to leave an understanding of *how to handle* that inheritance from a pragmatic perspective, which is the wisdom and financial acumen to properly handle monetary blessings. Otherwise, your children will spend the inheritance and will have nothing left to leave to *their* kids and grandkids.

God has called us to "pass it on" to our children and to their children and on down the line. Are you passing it on? Are you investing into the lives of the next generation so that they will have a biblical understanding of these financial matters?

If you want to hear God say to you one day, "Well done, good and faithful servant" (Matt. 25:21-23; Luke 19:17), then take seriously this responsibility to care for the next generation. Our children are too valuable an asset to do anything less.

Time for a Change

If for no other reason, we've got to help our little boys and girls understand that it's not about brain power, it's not about ethnicity, it's not about what side of the track they're from: Life is about growing up to be what God calls them to be. (Then they can buy their own track!) The only way to do this is by taking care of business and financial affairs God's way, and passing this teaching on to our kids.

The measure of my ministry is not seen in me alone. The measure of my ministry is in my *children's children*. My son and daughters are only one generation. I've got to speak something into their spirits that they can turn and speak into their sons' and daughters' generation.

Diligent investing and making your money count is a Kingdom principle established by God Himself. He has laid out a clear process for us to follow to take care of business until Jesus returns. *If* you and your family are worth the effort and *if* you desire to learn God's process governing financial and monetary affairs, begin with a decision to put His process into practice and to handle your monetary affairs God's way! A "good" man or woman receives and releases—starting with the next generation.

The choice is yours.

Poverty is the result of our refusal to share with others. Even God will not force us to do good. We must choose to do the good.

MOTHER TERESA

Chapter 19

So . . . How Much?

So here comes the question of the day: *How much is enough?* With the kind of theology that has crept into the Body of Christ today, that is a question that is rarely (if ever) asked. How much is enough?

Remember what abundance is: the surplus of a fixed measurement. You will never be in abundance until you define how much is enough. Jesus Christ died owning nothing material but His tunic. Mother Teresa died owning nothing. Dr. Bill Bright, a man whom I've known and who mentored me from afar, died owning nothing. Yet, they all gave in massive ways—both financially and spiritually.

One thing people seem to forget is that the Bible was not written for Americans and the American money mind-set alone. People think that someone like Mother Teresa, who only owned a couple of slippers and a robe, was poor. But wealth is not necessarily cash or income or bank balances. Mother Teresa, who had virtually zero of her own property, could command a jet aircraft at her disposal with a single phone call if she wanted to. She was as wealthy and as prosperous as God had ordained her to be in the position where He put her. And even though she was seemingly "poor" by our Western mind-set, she helped tens of thousands of people while she was alive—the homeless, the sick, the lame—and all with no possessions of her own. She was truly rich in the Lord, because she was where God wanted her to be, doing what He wanted her to be doing, helping people who needed to be helped in ways that challenge American monetary convention.

The Bible was written for all people—Africans, Pakistanis, Chinese, Indians, Americans, and on and on—so it has to be taken in the context that it was written. In the context of Kolkata (Calcutta), India, one of the most densely populated and poorest cities in the entire world, a nun doesn't build corporations—yet she can still give significantly. Mother Teresa did things that a man like Bill Gates could not do, because she had the spiritual riches from which to draw (which included relationships with powerful and wealthy people). She may not have had the cash, but she had a level of respect, connections and international reputation that crossed all borders and ethnic, cultural and sociopolitical divisions, allowing her to get things done on a worldwide scale. Men such as Paul Allen, Warren Buffet, Ted Turner or Bill Gates might be able to write huge checks, but Mother Teresa's reach, influence and effect were every bit as far, deep and wide as theirs.

Another example is Dr. Bill Bright. He also died owning nothing. When Dr. Bright was a college student, he made a covenant with God that he would own no possessions and would trust God with everything. People teased Bill about wearing the same black suit all the time. He didn't own a thing. He gave his life for the kingdom of God. He gave his life for others. And for the last eight or ten years of his life, Dr. Bright traveled in a private jet. A billionaire made it available to him.

But there's a huge flip side. I was honored to co-chair the last Billy Graham Crusade in Los Angeles in November 2004, along with my dearest friends Dr. Jack Hayford and Dr. Lloyd Ogilvie. On the Sunday prior to the crusade, I sat in a meeting in which Dr. Billy Graham was presented with the Prince of Peace Award. Only three other people had ever received it: King Hussein of Jordan, Egyptian President Anwar Sadat and Mother Teresa—and then, Dr. Billy Graham. It was a beautiful statue, and along with it came a cash gift of half a million dollars. On the spot, upon receiving the money, Dr. Billy Graham donated it all to the crusade where 7,000 people would make life-changing decisions during the presentation of the gospel of Jesus Christ. At that same meeting, there was a man sitting in the front row, and we shared with him that we were almost two million dollars behind in the budget for that particular crusade. Right then and there, the man wrote a personal check for another half a million dollars.

There is a principle that we need to learn, and if we miss it, we will admire the fact that Mother Teresa and Bill Bright died with nothing, much more than we will admire men who are able to give away a half a million dollars to do God's work without batting an eyelash. Money counts when we become rivers and channels of blessing rather than reservoirs of wealth. All of these saints–Mother Teresa, Bill Bright, Billy Graham and the donor at the crusade–gave to God's kingdom. But Billy Graham and the donor gave out of God's *overflow.* Imagine what is in the cup of men who can so easily and readily gave away a half a million dollars on the spot!

Do not get caught up in some holy poverty mentality that makes you think you're more spiritual if you're more broke. God speaks to our hearts. There's a calling that He has on each of our lives. For some of us, it's a call to make do on a more meager income and to give of ourselves as abundance to others. For others, it's a call to have resources and the ability to write large checks, to sow into the Kingdom, to sponsor the show, to pay for the costumes, to buy the bread, to pay the salaries to bless charities and other worthwhile humanitarian causes. It is only a spirit of mammon that brings a poverty mentality. That's the difference between simply giving and giving out of God's overflow.

God can and does create millionaires. There are many Christian millionaires in training, not because they're super-spiritual, but because they will sit under the Word of God and honor Him and get into a position to be blessed. He knows He can trust them with His riches. There is a word that goes beyond wealth, beyond money, even beyond riches, and that word is "prosperity." God desires prosperity for you so that you can turn around and give to the needs of His kingdom.

Chapter 19

The Great Choreographer

Each year since 1947, Tony Awards have been awarded for various categories of theatrical stage presentation. Best Performance. Best Orchestration. Best Costume. Also included in the list is Best Choreography, for the person who orchestrates the best dance sequence in a musical or Broadway show.

God is the great choreographer of life. He would win the Tony every year if they'd let Him enter the contest. And when it comes to financial matters and the use of money and resources, God is also the choreographer behind it all. He's there when the seed is first sown, all the way through to the very end when it is multiplied and passed along to others.

> Now he that ministereth seed to the sower both minister bread for your food, and multiply your seed sown, and increase the fruits of your righteousness (2 Cor. 9:10, *KJV*).

The word "ministereth" is the Greek word *epichoregeo*, which is the word from which we get our word "choreography." The prefix "epi" means *upon*, and the root word "choregeo" means *to be a dance leader*. When the two parts of the word are put together, the end result means to supply the needs of, to furnish, to fully supply, to aid or contribute, to add to, or to minister to. To *choreograph*.

The entire process outlined in 2 Corinthians 9:6-11 is orchestrated, or *choreographed*, by our God. Watch the way Paul divides up the 2 Corinthians 9:10 verse: He says God gives us seed for *food* and that He gives us seed for *sowing*. In other words, the same God who gives us bread for eating also gives us seed for sowing. "Bread" symbolizes our need. The catch is in the word "ministereth." The *New International Version* says "supplies." Other versions say "gives." Whatever the translation, the point is that God supplies seed for sowing *and* gives us bread for eating.

You can't separate the two—they go hand in hand. But God does not *make* bread. He gives us the seed and helps us to harvest it so that *we* do the making of the actual bread—which only happens after we've sown the seed and the seed has brought forth a harvest. *We* must harvest the seed. *We* must turn the seed from the harvest into flour. *We* must mix the flour into dough. *We* must put the dough into the heat of the oven. And then, when things cool down . . . *voilà!*: bread. God gives us everything we need to get bread, but *we* have to *make the bread*.

There's a process to get from seed to bread, and God is the *choreographer* behind that process. God supplies—it is He who "ministereth." In other words, He is the conductor, sponsor, financer of a chorus that performs. It's a great picture of what happens in the artistic world, like a troupe of performers going around from place to place: The one who supplies is the one who backs the troupe, the one who pays all the bills for the performance. In the 2 Corinthians 9 passage, the one who supplies the needs of the performers is the word that is used for *God*. Here's what God does: He's the one who's in charge of all the details, so that when it's time for the actors and performers to take center stage, everything they need in order to perform at their optimum has already been taken care of by Somebody behind the scenes, whom the people out front never see. That Somebody is God.

God is the supplier of the seed that you plant for sowing, and something has to happen for the seed to become bread. All that the people (the audience, those around us, the world) see is the bread—the performance—but Somebody works behind the scenes to choreograph the process from a little seed all the way to a full performance.

Somebody tells the sower when to sow.

Somebody prepares the ground to receive the seed.

Somebody puts the nutrients in the soil to receive the seed.

Somebody tells the rain when to fall on the soil that's prepared to receive this seed.

Somebody tells the sower when to pull the weeds out of the soil.

Somebody tells the grain when it's time to receive the harvest.

Somebody grinds up the wheat seeds to turn the grain into flour.

Somebody tells the sower how much water to add to the flour, when to put it in the oven, how long to bake it, when to take it out, and suddenly . . . bread.

God has been working behind the scenes every step of the way, but people look at you and all they see is bread. You're wearing bread. Driving a shiny new loaf of bread. Living in a big bread box. They don't know all that God had to do in your life to bring you all that bread! They don't know what God had to rearrange and pre-arrange. They don't know what God had to put into place and avoid and fix and move and cajole and balance and smooth and hide and reveal and swing and smash and build up and tear down and repair! They don't know what kind of obstacles God had to bring you through. All they know is that you came out of the oven smellin' *good*, in the name of Jesus! God has been in action behind the scenes the whole time, giving you what you need. He's been there saying, "Okay, if you sow the seed, I'll make sure the seed brings forth a harvest. I'll do My steps, and you do yours."

God grants the seed to sow, and we're to take that seed and do two things with it: eat some of it and replant or re-sow the rest.

Always remember: God's goal is not merely to meet *your* need. He is not seeking mere sufficiency for *you*. His goal is abundance so that you can shower your overflow onto *others*.

It is amazing to know that orchestrating from behind the scenes on our behalf to see to it that the process is as smooth and successful as possible is God, Creator of the universe! I am constantly astounded by the depth of the love of God, and humbled by the knowledge that He loves me. That is a revelation that has become the very motivation and inspiration for my life. If you get nothing else out of this book, simply get this: *Know that God loves you.* He doesn't care what you've done. He doesn't care where you've been. God woke you up this morning and, as my grandmother used to say, "touched you with a finger of love." He allowed you to see a day you've never seen before and shall never see again, for one reason and one reason only: because He loves you! He knows you—and still He loves you.

There are some people who know me but don't love me. Everyone has people in their lives who know them but don't love them. Then there are others who love me but don't truly *know* me. No doubt you've got some of those, too. But God is so much God that He knows me and loves me anyway! I don't care what people said about you, I don't care what you've been involved in, I don't care what names they've called you, I don't care what you've done, I don't care what you've been—God loves you.

I realize that this is Spirituality 101 for most Christians, but stick with me for a minute here. As you read these words, I'm going ask you to say something out loud—and I give you fair warning, when you say these words, it might feel uncomfortable for you. Yet it is a revelation of truth that God would plant into your spirit. Say this out loud right now: "God loves me."

Say it again: "God loves me!"

Now say it this way: "God loves *me*."

For some people, saying that causes a tug in the gut that is uncomfortable, because they don't really feel it. They think of all they've done, and the statement just seems too unbelievable. Yet, the truth remains: God *does* love you. The God who loves you is the Source of your life and the Source of the provisions for your life. The very essence of God is that God is love (see 1 John 4:8,16). And because He loves, He releases blessings into your life.

Make Your Money Count!

Humility and the fear of the Lord bring wealth and honor and life.

Proverbs 22:4, *NIV*

Some church folk are the most selfish people I've ever met. We don't even hear much talk about missions nowadays—not like we did in the 1950s through the 1970s. All you hear about these days is who's got the biggest this and who's got the most that. I'm not demeaning or denouncing material possessions. Not at all. I'm talking about where our *hearts* are. What drives our lives? Are we driven by seed, by need or by greed?

If you're going to have a heart that beats like Christ, you're going to have a heart after God's own heart. God is going to take you from the place of wanting to have your needs met, to a place where you need to find somebody else's needs to meet. Maybe God is trying to put you into a position where you look for places to bless people. For some of us, maybe God has blessed us to put our sons or daughters through college. Others struggle to put their kids through school. And perhaps others have received scholarships. If you've sent your son or daughter through college, maybe God wants you to help put somebody else's son or daughter through school. Could it be? Maybe God is trying to get you to a place where you're able to write the check and sow into the Kingdom and advance the gospel in tangible, physical ways.

When we are living obediently, we will live in God's overflow. I don't know about you, but I want to live in the overflow. I want to live where the abundance that God gives me is at *God's disposal*!

Many people know the pain and the frustration of being in a worship service or some other situation where God speaks to their heart and they have the desire to sow or to help someone, but when they look in their wallet or purse or check their bank account, God reminds them how they just wasted $300 last week. And it hits home: If they had that $300 now, they could bless somebody with it! Now all they can do is pray for that need. Don't get me wrong—prayers are essential! They're important to give, they are crucial, but as James once said:

> What good is it, my brothers, if a man claims to have faith but has no deeds? Can such faith save him? Suppose a brother or sister is without clothes and daily food. If one of you says to him, "Go, I wish you well; keep warm and well fed," but does nothing about his physical needs, what good is it? (Jas. 2:14-16, *NIV*).

Peter was a fisherman. He owned a boat. One day Jesus asked Peter to give Him that boat to preach from. Jesus had need of it. Peter gave it.

When Jesus got ready to walk into Jerusalem for the last time on His way to Calvary, He told a man, "Tell them 'Jesus has needs of your donkey.'" God had need of it. The man gave it.

You know where I want to be? I want to be so far in the overflow that when God says, "I have need of your resources to bless this person over here," I can bless them. I want to be able to write that check! I want to be able to supply their need. I want to be able to sponsor them. I want to be able to help them become what God has called them to be. I want to live in the overflow and set an example of what God can do with a willing heart and an obedient spirit.

> Thou preparest the table before me in the presence of my enemies; thou anointest my head with oil; my cup runneth over (Ps. 23:5, *KJV*).

Have you ever thought about what would happen if one of your enemies was at the party when God started preparing a table before you, and that enemy was standing close while your cup was running over? I'm talking about God blessing you with so much overflow that you end up blessing the people around you who have cursed you! Blessing those who didn't want to see you blessed! Blessing people who tried to hold you back! Blessing people who said you'd never make it and claimed you'd never amount to anything. God wants to bless you so much that you bless some folks who didn't even want to see you blessed.

Don't you want to live in the overflow for the sake of the Kingdom? Don't you want to draw closer to God and live your life in His constant presence? He is our sole and abundant Source. He gives you seed and He gives you bread. And then He multiplies the seed and keeps on giving you bread.

But there are steps along the way to doing what God has called us to do in dealing properly with our money until He returns. If you want to hear, "Well done, My good and faithful servant," then be ready to get down to business. The degree of your blessings all depends on your response to the question, "Will you start making your money count God's way?"

Blessed is the man that walketh not in the counsel of the ungodly, nor standeth in the way of sinners, nor sitteth in the seat of the scornful. But his delight is in the law of the LORD*; and in his law doth he meditate day and night. And he shall be like a tree planted by the rivers of water, that bringeth forth his fruit in his season; his leaf also shall not wither; and whatsoever he doeth shall prosper.*

PSALM 1:1-3, *KJV*

Acknowledgments

Pulling together a book like this is much like staging a theatrical production—it can never move from dream to reality without the help of countless hours invested by a host of people involved in bringing it to fruition.

I want to express my deep gratitude to the following people for their belief, support and contributions to this project:

To Michael McCall, my partner in the writing ministry, who has the unique ability to say what I think and who always sees beyond my thoughts. Your gift of communication inspires me to inspire others.

To Derrick Wade, my friend and colleague, whose insight into the promotion and marketing dimensions of the entertainment industry has contributed to the distribution of this project.

To Marvin Johnson, my faithful assistant, who thinks of stuff I don't think of (and even when I do, I still sometimes forget!).

To Charles Brooks, who runs the church while I try to pastor it.

To the staff of Faithful Central Bible Church, which is an extension of my passion to pastor.

To Gary Greig, Steven Lawson and the tremendous staff at Regal Books for welcoming me to the Regal family and for their belief in this project.

About the Author

Dr. Kenneth C. Ulmer has been pastor of Faithful Central Bible Church (formerly Faithful Central Missionary Baptist Church) in Inglewood, California, since January 1982. During his tenure, the congregation has grown from 350 to nearly 14,000, and now occupies the Great Western Forum, previous home of the Los Angeles Lakers professional basketball team.

Dr. Ulmer received his Bachelor of Arts degree in Broadcasting & Music from the University of Illinois. After accepting his call to the ministry, Dr. Ulmer was ordained at Mount Moriah Missionary Baptist Church in Los Angeles. His has studied at Pepperdine University, Hebrew Union College, the University of Judaism and Christ Church and Wadham College at Oxford University in England. In June 1986, he received a Ph.D. from Grace Graduate School of Theology, in Long Beach, California (which became the West Coast Campus of Grace Theological Seminary). In June 1989, he was awarded an Honorary Doctor of Divinity from Southern California School of Ministry, and in May 1999 he received his Doctor of Ministry from United Theological Seminary.

In 1994, Dr. Ulmer was consecrated Bishop of Christian Education of the Full Gospel Baptist Church Fellowship, where he sat on the Bishops' Council. He has served on the Board of Directors of the Gospel Music Workshop of America, the Pastor's Advisory Council for the City of Inglewood, and the Board of Trustees of Southern California School of Ministry.

In early 2000, Dr. Ulmer was installed as the Presiding Bishop over the Macedonia International Bible Fellowship, with churches representing the countries of Zimbabwe, Namibia, Angola, Republic of the Congo, South Africa and the United States.

Dr. Ulmer has served as a council member of the California Attorney General's Policy Council on Violence Prevention and as a member of the Board of Directors of the Rebuild Los Angeles (RLA) Committee. He participated in the study of Ecumenical Liturgy and Worship at Magdalene College at Oxford University in England, has served as an instructor in Pastoral Ministry and Homiletics at Grace Theological Seminary, as an instructor of African-American Preaching at Fuller Theological Seminary in Pasadena, as an adjunct professor at Biola University (where he served on the Board of Trustees), and as an adjunct professor at Pepperdine University. He is currently an adjunct professor at The King's College and Seminary in Los Angeles (where he is also a founding board member).

Dr. Ulmer is an accomplished writer and published author of three previous books: *A New Thing* (a reflection on the Full Gospel Baptist Movement), *Spiritually Fit to Run the Race* (a guide to godly living) and *In His Image: An Intimate Reflection of God* (an update of his book, *The Anatomy of God*).

Dr. Ulmer and his wife, residents of Los Angeles, California, have been married for 30 years and have three daughters, one son and five grandchildren.

Other Books and Products by Kenneth C. Ulmer, Ph.D.

In His Image:
An Intimate Reflection of God
(Whitaker House, 2005)
Spiritually Fit to Run the Race:
A Personal Training Manual for Godly Living
(Nashville, TN: Thomas Nelson, 1999)
The New Spirit-Filled Life Bible:
Kingdom Equipping Through the Power of the Word
(co-editor)
(Nashville, TN: Thomas Nelson, 2006)
The Bible Experience (audio book)
(voice for the book of Ephesians)
(Grand Rapids, MI, 2006)

Messages Related to Making Your Money Count:
The Challenge of Real Worship (six-part CD series)
Money Matters (four-part CD series)
Living in the Circle (two-part CD series)

Dr. Ulmer has other messages and teachings available on CD and DVD that can be purchased through the following:

Faithful Central Bible Church
333 W. Florence Avenue
Inglewood, CA 90301

Faithfulcentral.com